Insider's Guide to the Paris 2024 Summer Olympics:
Your Unofficial Guide to Venues, Transportation, Dining, Accommodation, and Everything You Need to Know

By Brian Winters

Copyright © 2024 Brian Winters. All rights reserved.

This publication is protected under copyright law. Reproduction or distribution of any portion of this book, in any form or by any means—whether electronic, mechanical, photocopying, recording, or through any information storage and retrieval system—is prohibited without the express written consent of the publisher, except as allowed by law.

Disclaimer

This book is intended to serve as a general resource on the Olympic Games. Although the author has diligently sought to provide accurate information, he expressly disclaims responsibility for any losses, damages, or disruptions caused by inaccuracies or omissions, regardless of whether they result from negligence, accidents, or any other cause. The strategies and advice presented may not fit every circumstance. It is recommended that readers consult with qualified professionals for tailored guidance. Neither the author nor the publisher assumes any legal liability or responsibility for any consequences, harm, or other outcomes that may result from using the information in this book.

Trademarks, product names, logos, and brands mentioned within this book belong to their respective owners and are used for identification purposes only. Their mention does not signify any association with this book, nor does it imply endorsement or sponsorship.

The terms and symbols associated with the Olympic Games, including the Olympic rings, are trademarks of the International Olympic Committee (IOC). Their use in this book is strictly for educational and informational aims and does not suggest any endorsement by or association with the IOC.

About the Author

Brian Winters' zeal for sports has been a constant throughout his life, with a particular adoration for the Olympic Games that began in his early years. The unforgettable highlights of the 1992 Barcelona Games were the catalyst for his enduring interest in the narratives and achievements of elite athletes worldwide. Brian's journey has led him to witness the Olympic Games in person on numerous occasions, allowing him to absorb the essence of this monumental event from an insider's vantage point. His travels and direct observations have equipped him with a deep understanding of the Olympics' complex dynamics.

Beyond his role as an Olympic aficionado, Brian is a distinguished sports journalist and writer. His contributions to various sports media outlets have been recognized for their thorough analysis, compelling narratives, and dedication to truthful and riveting reportage. Through this guidebook, Brian aspires to impart his extensive knowledge and firsthand accounts, guiding readers through an intimate exploration of the Olympic Games. He delves into the event's storied past, cultural significance, operational intricacies, and the personal journeys of the athletes, crafting an essential compendium for both long-time followers and newcomers to the preeminent sports competition. Outside of his Olympic-focused endeavors, Brian is often found rooting for his favorite sports teams and athletes or embarking on new journeys to feed his Olympic passion.

Table of Contents

About the Author	5
Table of Contents	7
Welcome to the Olympics!	**11**
Overview of this guidebook	11
Bonjour, Paris! Embracing the Olympic Spirit	13
History of the Games	13
Why Paris for the Olympics?	15
The Olympic spirit: Fair play, respect, and friendship	16
The Tokyo 2020 Olympics: A look back	17
Olympic Games and France Hosting History	**21**
Paris: A Historic Olympic Host	21
Legacy of Previous Olympic Games in France	22
Paris 2024: Preparations and Challenges	**24**
Overview of paris 2024 preparation	24
Mascot	25
Progress on infrastructure projects	26
Sustainability initiatives planned for the Games	28
Security measures and contingency planning	29
All About the Sports	**30**
New sports debuting in Paris 2024	30
Brief explanations and rules of each sport	36
Archery	36
Athletics	37
Badminton	37
Basketball	38
3x3 Basketball	39
Boxing	39
Canoe Slalom	40
Canoe sprint	40
Road cycling	41
Track cycling	42
BMX freestyle	42
BMX racing	43

Equestrian	44
Fencing	45
Soccer	45
Artistic gymnastics	46
Rhythmic gymnastics	47
Trampolining	48
Handball	48
Hockey	49
Judo	49
Modern pentathlon	50
Rowing	51
Rugby	51
Sailing	52
Shooting	53
Table tennis	53
Taekwondo	54
Tennis	54
Triathlon	55
Volleyball	55
Beach volleyball	56
Diving	56
Marathon swimming	57
Artistic swimming	57
Swimming	57
Water polo	59
Weightlifting	60
Wrestling	60
Star athletes to watch and their stories	61
Attending the Games in Paris	**65**
Ticketing Information: Securing Your Seat at the Paris 2024 Games	65
Venues: Locations, access, and amenities	67
Paris Regions	69
Grand Palais	69
Alexandre III Bridge	70
Porte de la Chapelle Arena	70
Parc Urbain La Concorde	70

The Trocadéro	71
The Eiffel Tower Stadium	71
Les Invalides	72
The Cour d'Honneur	72
The Champ de Mars	73
Roland-Garros	73
The Parc des Princes	74
South Paris Arena	74
Hôtel de Ville	76
Bercy Arena	76
Île-de-France regions	78
Yves-du-Manoir Stadium	78
Paris La Défense Arena	79
Aquatics Centre	80
Stade de France	80
Le Bourget Sport Climbing Venue	81
North Paris Arena	82
Vaires-sur-Marne Nautical Stadium	82
Château de Versailles	83
Elancourt Hill	84
Saint-Quentin-en-Yvelines BMX Stadium	84
Saint-Quentin-en-Yvelines Vélodrome	85
Golf National	86
Beyond Paris	87
Pierre Mauroy Stadium	87
La Beaujoire Stadium	88
Châteauroux Shooting Centre	88
Lyon Stadium	89
Geoffroy-Guichard Stadium	90
Bordeaux Stadium	90
Nice Stadium	91
Marseille Stadium	91
Marseille Marina	92
Teahupo'o	92
Spectator etiquette and guidelines	93
Budgeting for the Games in Paris	**96**

Accommodation options: Hotels, hostels, and alternatives	96
Food and dining options: Restaurants, cafes, and on-site options	115
Transportation costs and planning specific to Paris	135
Packing Essentials for Paris	**141**
Weather and climate considerations (clothing and gear)	142
Health and Safety Essentials for the Paris 2024 Olympics	145
Staying Safe and Healthy in Paris	**148**
General Health and Safety Tips for Travelers in Paris	149
Staying Informed: Resources for Official Updates	151
Cultural Exchange Tips and Overcoming Language Barriers	152
Celebrating Diversity and Sportsmanship at the Olympics	154
Appendices	**157**
Important Contact Information: Paris 2024 Olympic Games	157
Appendix B: Maps	160
Map 1: Charles De Gaulle Airport to Eiffel tower	160
Map 2: Olympic Venues in Paris	161
Map 3: Restaurants	161
Map 4: Activities	162
Map 5: ATMs	162

Welcome to the Olympics!

Overview of this guidebook

Introducing your all-encompassing handbook for the Paris 2024 Olympic and Paralympic Games! Flip through these pages and you'll uncover everything necessary to fully enjoy this epic occasion. Whether it's the adrenaline-pumping athletic showdowns or the vibrant cultural celebrations, whether you're strolling through Parisian boulevards or delving into the Games' lasting impact, we're here to ensure you're well-prepared.

Think of this guidebook not just as a trove of facts but as your ticket to the center of the excitement, your guide to adventure, and your trusty companion on this unforgettable odyssey. It doesn't matter if you're an Olympic aficionado or a newcomer to the festivities; there's a treasure trove of experiences waiting for you.

Here's a sneak peek at what's in store:

Insider Insights: Receive the freshest updates on the Paris 2024 happenings, from venue progress to personal tales of athletes gearing up for their big moment.

Practical Tips: Master the art of navigating Paris with ease, thanks to our essential advice on getting around, finding accommodations, dining out, and beyond. We're here to ensure your Olympic journey is smooth and worry-free.

Cultural Highlights: Dive into the essence of French culture with our selection of the top cultural happenings, festivals, and attractions coinciding with the Games. Experience Paris in a way you never have before, with its unique sights, sounds, and tastes.

Athlete Profiles: Meet the champions vying for triumph in Paris 2024. Discover the newcomers and the experienced contenders, their motivational stories, and their drive to excel in the global arena.

Legacy and Impact: Uncover the enduring significance of the Paris 2024 Olympics and their transformative effect on Paris, France, and the international community. See how the Games transcend sports to foster positive change and evolution.

Interactive Features: Engage with the Olympic experience through interactive maps, quizzes, and activities that promise fun for readers of all ages. Test your Olympic knowledge, follow your top athletes, and stumble upon Paris's hidden wonders.Introducing your all-encompassing handbook for the Paris 2024 Olympic and Paralympic Games! Flip through these pages and you'll uncover everything necessary to fully enjoy this epic occasion. Whether it's the adrenaline-pumping athletic showdowns or the vibrant cultural celebrations, whether you're strolling through Parisian boulevards or delving into the Games' lasting impact, we're here to ensure you're well-prepared.

Think of this guidebook not just as a trove of facts but as your ticket to the center of the excitement, your guide to adventure, and your trusty companion on this unforgettable odyssey. It doesn't matter if you're an Olympic aficionado or a newcomer to the festivities; there's a treasure trove of experiences waiting for you.

Bonjour, Paris! Embracing the Olympic Spirit

Picture this: the buzz of electricity in the air, the thunderous applause from the stands, and the crème de la crème of athletes stretching their abilities to the utmost on what can only be described as the ultimate global platform. That's the scene set for the 2024 Paris Olympics, an event poised to outshine anything France, or indeed the planet, has witnessed before.

Circle the dates from July 26th to August 11th, 2024, on your calendar, because Paris is gearing up to become the heartbeat of international sports and festivities. But it's not just about who's the fastest or the strongest; it's a celebration of cultures: a colorful mosaic crafted from the many threads of different traditions and sporting excellence.

Prepare to be carried away by the indelible vibe of the Olympic ethos. Be part of history as elite competitors vie for top honors, stamping their legacy on the global platform. Dive into the charged ambiance with other enthusiastic supporters from across the world, all speaking the universal language of sportsmanship and friendship.

This event is more than just athleticism on display; it's a shared journey that crosses all divides. It's an opportunity to be at the forefront of human achievement, to embrace our varied backgrounds, and to create lasting memories. So, get your gear ready, awaken your inner victor, and get set to be captivated by the wonders of the Paris Olympics! Strap in for an escapade that's too good to pass up.

History of the Games

The Olympics serve as an enduring symbol of how sports can bring people together, creating a shared story that crosses time, land, and different ways of life. As we move toward the excitement of the Paris 2024 Olympics, it's essential to explore the deep and colorful history of the Olympic saga, a tale as majestic as old myths and as vibrant as contemporary dreams.

Back to the Start

The grand story of the Olympics dates back more than 2,700 years to the sunny landscapes of ancient Greece, with the first documented Games in 776 BCE. In the peaceful grounds of Olympia, these initial competitions were a lively homage to physical skill and honor, drawing athletes from the Greek realm to compete in various challenges, from running and wrestling to chariot racing and discus. For those Greeks, the Olympics were more than a contest; they were a holy celebration in honor of Zeus that promoted unity, friendship, and truce among the city-states.

A New Chapter for the Olympics

After a long period of silence, the Olympic spirit was reawakened in the 19th century by the forward-thinking French educator Pierre de Coubertin. He was moved by the enduring essence of the ancient Games and aspired to create a modern Olympic movement that would bridge divides and foster peace and friendship across nations. His vision became a reality with the first modern Olympic Games in Athens, Greece, in 1896, signaling the revival of an age-old tradition and the start of a worldwide sensation.

Growth and Diversification

Since then, the Olympic Games have grown and diversified, reflecting the changing tides of history while keeping their eternal charm. The Olympics now include a wide array of sports, showcasing the vast scope of human skill and ambition. Each Olympic event brings new records, new champions, and new tales of victory and resilience that enthrall people everywhere.

Highs and Lows

Olympic history is marked by unforgettable highs and profound lows, moments that resonate through time and touch our collective memory. From Jesse Owens' iconic wins in 1936, challenging the shadows of Nazi beliefs, to the "Miracle on Ice" in 1980, embodying American determination, these instances shine as beacons of hope in a sometimes gloomy world. But the Olympics have faced tough times too, like the Munich tragedy in 1972 and the Games cancellations during World War II, reminding us that peace and unity are delicate in our ever-shifting world.

Enduring Influence

The impact of the Olympic Games goes beyond the sparkle of the competitions. They leave a lasting mark through iconic venues, technological advancements, and the cultural ties and friendships formed between countries. The Olympics spark urban rejuvenation, economic growth, and social advancement, leaving a legacy of motivation, creativity, and inclusiveness that echoes long after the medals are handed out.

Eyes on the Future

Looking ahead to the Paris 2024 Olympics, we build on the legacy of those who laid the groundwork for these upcoming Games. The story goes on, and the world eagerly anticipates the next installment in the Olympic narrative—a story filled with optimism, grit, and an unwavering belief in the transformative power of sports to improve lives, bring nations together, and inspire future generations. The stage is ready, the flame is burning, and the Olympic spirit is alive and well. Let's embark on this new adventure.

Why Paris for the Olympics?

Paris, affectionately known as the City of Light, shines as a beacon of culture, history, and forward-thinking—a city that has enchanted the globe for ages. But why is Paris the dream location for the Olympic Games? Let's dive into the standout traits and persuasive arguments that position Paris as the ideal backdrop for the upcoming Olympics.

Experience in Hosting Olympics and Infrastructure

France boasts a storied legacy of hosting the Olympics, having done so with flair in 1900 and 1924, showcasing its capability and know-how in organizing grand sports events.

Ready-made infrastructure: Paris is equipped with renowned stadiums, a robust transport network, and plenty of lodging options. This ready-to-go infrastructure cuts down on the need for new construction, saving money and ensuring everything is set to go.

Vision and Dedication

Paris stepped up with an ambitious and convincing proposal for the 2024 Games, emphasizing eco-friendliness, inclusivity, and cutting-edge innovation. This proposal struck a chord with the International Olympic Committee (IOC) and its ideals.

Government backing: The French authorities have pledged strong support and financial investment in the Games, cementing Paris's position as a strong contender.

Strategic Position and Worldwide Impact

Ease of access and visitor appeal: Nestled in the heart of Europe, Paris is a breeze to get to for athletes, officials, and fans worldwide. The city's deep cultural roots and status as a must-visit spot add to its allure.

Economic perks: The Olympics promise to rev up the French economy with increased tourism, job opportunities, and infrastructure upgrades, fueling long-term prosperity.

Alignment with ongoing projects

Paris's Olympic proposal was in harmony with current national projects focused on green practices and nurturing young talent, highlighting a dedication to societal ambitions that go beyond just the Games. The 2024 Olympics will mark 100 years since the 1924 Paris Games, offering a special chance to honor this milestone and leave a lasting mark.

It's crucial to remember that the selection process was multifaceted. Although the reasons mentioned here were influential, the ultimate choice likely involved a nuanced mix of many elements.

The Olympic spirit: Fair play, respect, and friendship

At the heart of the Olympic ethos, there's a trio of timeless principles that go beyond mere athletics—these are the ideals that capture the true nature of our shared humanity. We're talking about the pillars of fair play, respect, and friendship, which form the foundation of that unique Olympic vibe, motivating both athletes and fans to aim high, treat each other with honor, and create friendships that know no borders.

Fair Play

Let's chat about fair play: It's not just about following the rules; it's an attitude, a belief system, a way of approaching life. It means playing with a sense of integrity, truthfulness, and fair competition, always respecting the game's rules and the essence of competing. It's about putting in your all, whether you win or lose, and handling the results with poise and self-respect. In a world where winning at all costs seems to be the mantra, fair play nudges us to remember that the real win is in playing with heart and sincerity.

Respect

Now, when it comes to respect, it's the glue that holds any solid relationship together, be it on the field or out in the big wide world. It's about acknowledging everyone's value and dignity, no matter who they are or where they come from. On the Olympic stage, respect shows up in various ways—it's in the pre-game handshakes, the clapping for a great opponent, the salute to another athlete's triumphs. It's all about treating folks with kindness, empathy, and care, creating a space where everyone feels welcome and understood.

Friendship

And let's not forget friendship—it's the pulse of the Olympic movement, connecting athletes, fans, and countries in a common quest for greatness and togetherness. It's about building relationships based on trust and respect, looking past our differences in language, culture, and nationality. In the Olympic village, friendships take root among competitors who might've been total strangers, brought together by their passion for sports and their Olympic-sized ambitions. These are the friendships that stick around after the medals have been handed out, reminding us of sports' incredible ability to unite folks in a spirit of harmony and fellowship.

As we gear up for the Paris 2024 Olympics, let's fully embrace these core values of fair play, respect, and friendship that are so central to the Olympic spirit. Let's celebrate the athletes who live out these ideals and fill us with awe through their bravery, perseverance, and elegance. And let's not forget that it's not just about snagging the most medals—it's about living out the Olympic spirit and creating a legacy of honesty, respect, and friendship for the future.

The Tokyo 2020 Olympics: A look back

As we gear up for the Paris 2024 Olympics, let's pause to remember the Tokyo 2020 Olympics, a truly unique event in the annals of sports. The athletes' stunning feats and the remarkable success of holding such an event during a global health crisis have left an everlasting impression on the world of sports and beyond.

Battling the Odds

The journey to the Tokyo 2020 Olympics was filled with unprecedented challenges due to the COVID-19 pandemic. Despite the odds, Tokyo shined, showcasing incredible strength, grit, and an unwavering dedication to delivering a safe and memorable Games. The organizers' commitment shone through as they implemented strict health measures and overcame numerous logistical challenges, proving their exceptional tenacity in tough times.

Moments to Remember

Looking back at the Tokyo 2020 Olympics, it's hard to forget the remarkable moments and stellar performances that made the Games so special. From the awe-inspiring athletic displays to the touching victories, Tokyo 2020 was an event to remember for years.

Simone Biles, the American gymnastics star, not only wowed us with her skills but also with her bravery and strength in facing mental health struggles. By choosing to step back from some events for her health, Biles sparked a global dialogue on mental wellness in sports and earned respect worldwide.

In the pool, Caeleb Dressel proved himself as one of the all-time swimming greats. The American swimmer bagged five golds and broke Olympic records, leaving fans in awe with his speed and flawless technique.

Norwegian hurdler Karsten Warholm stunned everyone in the men's 400m hurdles, breaking the world record with a time of 45.94 seconds. His gold medal run was a perfect example of what dedication and hard work can achieve.

Elaine Thompson-Herah from Jamaica made history by winning gold in both the 100m and 200m sprints in back-to-back Olympics. Her incredible pace and form confirmed her as one of the top female sprinters ever, showcasing the fruits of persistence and the quest for greatness.

Britain's Tom Daley touched hearts worldwide with his poignant victory in the men's synchronized 10m platform diving. After years of hard work, Daley and his partner Matty Lee seized gold, achieving a dream and leaving a lasting mark as one of Britain's diving legends. His emotional celebration and message of love and acceptance struck a chord with many, highlighting the significance of inclusivity in sports. These and many other unforgettable performances at Tokyo 2020 exemplified the strength of the human spirit and the pursuit of excellence. These moments remind us of how sports can inspire, bring people together, and elevate spirits globally.

Celebrating Diversity

The Tokyo 2020 Olympics was a vibrant display of diversity, with athletes from all over the world and from all walks of life shining bright. The Paralympians who broke records and the pioneering women who claimed victory showed the inclusive nature of the Olympic spirit. As competitors from various backgrounds united, they represented unity, respect, and solidarity—the core values of the Olympics. The Tokyo 2020 Olympics' legacy continues to echo, inspiring upcoming athletes and promoting global harmony. The Games have left a lasting impact of hope, resilience, and human triumph. Reflecting on Tokyo 2020, we're reminded of the unifying power of sports to overcome obstacles, bring people together, and create positive change.

Ultimately, the Tokyo 2020 Olympics were more than a competition; they were a tribute to the resilience of humanity, a festivity of endurance, and a beacon of hope during tough times. As we carry the lessons and memories from Tokyo 2020, let's stay motivated by the spirit of togetherness, determination, and solidarity as we anticipate the Paris 2024 Olympics and the future.

Olympic Games and France Hosting History

Paris: A Historic Olympic Host

Paris has long been a cornerstone in the Olympic saga, with a history drenched in time-honored customs, groundbreaking strides, and a relentless quest for greatness. Ever since the dawn of the modern Olympics, Paris has been instrumental in charting the course for this worldwide sports celebration. The city's influence stretches from its debut as host in 1900 to the eagerly anticipated 2024 Games, leaving a permanent imprint on the Olympics, and exemplifying the ideals of togetherness, diversity, and athletic skill.

Back in 1900, Paris opened its arms to the globe for the Olympics' second chapter. Although it was somewhat eclipsed by the simultaneous World's Fair, that event was a testament to Paris's dedication to global sports and set the stage for the city's future as a top Olympic venue. The 1924 Games in Paris bolstered this image, bringing to the table the first Olympic Village, the inaugural Olympic flame, and the introduction of the modern pentathlon.

As the 20th century rolled on, Paris didn't just rest on its laurels but continued to be the stage for numerous international sports events, like the Tour de France and the French Open. The city's famous sights — think the Eiffel Tower, the Champs-Élysées, and the Seine River — provided a breathtaking setting that heightened the Olympic thrill for both athletes and fans.

Paris even ventured into the winter sports arena, hosting the 1924 Winter Olympics in the neighboring Chamonix, highlighting France's knack for alpine skiing, figure skating, and ice hockey, and paving the way for more Winter Games to come in the country.

Fast forward to the 21st century, and Paris is once again in the spotlight, having clinched the opportunity to host the 2024 Summer Olympics and Paralympics. With its top-tier venues, commitment to eco-friendly practices, and a buzzing cultural vibe, Paris is all set to offer an unforgettable Olympic spectacle that honors its storied past and upholds the Olympic principles of fair competition, camaraderie, and mutual respect.

With the Paris 2024 Olympics on the horizon, the city is gearing up to roll out the red carpet for the world, ready to cast the spell of the Olympics on the biggest stage there is. Paris's illustrious Olympic history and its bright prospects are a shining example of the Games' lasting impact and the timeless spirit of the Olympic movement.

Legacy of Previous Olympic Games in France

France's history with the Olympics is truly unforgettable, leaving a mark on the country's culture and sports scene that lasts for ages. Each time France played host, it added to its rich Olympic tradition, influencing both its athletic identity and cultural fabric for years to come.

Back in 1900, the Paris Olympics were somewhat overshadowed by the big World's Fair event, but they still managed to set the stage for France's Olympic journey. Despite some hiccups and odd events like pigeon shooting, these Games put Paris on the map as a major player in the world of sports and culture, promoting a spirit of global friendship and paving the way for future Olympic adventures.

The 1924 Paris Olympics were a game-changer, bringing to life some amazing ideas like the first Olympic Village, the initial lighting of the Olympic flame, and the introduction of the modern pentathlon. These cool features not only made the Games more fun to watch but also raised the bar for all the future host cities. Plus, these Games were a symbol of France's determination and its dedication to rebuilding international bonds after the devastation of World War I.

France's adventures in the Winter Olympics kicked off with the 1924 Chamonix Winter Games. Set against the stunning French Alps, Chamonix was an ideal spot for the first-ever Winter Olympics, showing off France's skills in skiing, figure skating, and hockey, and cementing its status as a winter sports powerhouse.

Later Winter Olympics in France, like the ones in Grenoble in 1968 and Albertville in 1992, further boosted France's standing as a hotspot for winter sports fans. These events didn't just bring in the cash for the local areas but also left behind better facilities, more tourists, and a bigger spotlight on the international stage.

But it's not just about the sports. Hosting the Olympics has also sparked a wave of cultural creativity in France, leading to new artistic and architectural wonders, encouraging cultural exchanges, and stoking national pride. From the iconic Parisian venues to the charming rural landscapes, each Olympic event has been a chance to show off France's cultural richness and diversity to the entire world.

Now, with the Paris 2024 Olympics and Paralympics on the horizon, France is drawing on its impressive Olympic past for inspiration and drive. The country's history of hosting the Games is a shining example of its dedication to greatness, inclusiveness, and the Olympic values of friendship, respect, and fair play. Guided by this powerful legacy, France is all set to create an Olympic spectacle that's bound to captivate and bring together folks from across the globe.

Paris 2024: Preparations and Challenges

A century has passed since the Olympic flame last illuminated the Parisian sky. Now, in 2024, the City of Lights prepares to reignite the spirit of the Games, embarking on a journey filled with both meticulous preparations and anticipated challenges. This chapter delves into the intricate world surrounding the upcoming Paris Olympics, exploring the vision that guides its organization, the complexities of its preparation process, the potential hurdles that lie ahead, and the lasting impact it aims to leave on the world stage. We will delve into the ongoing preparations, examining the logistical complexities involved in hosting such a large-scale event. From infrastructure development and venue construction to transportation planning and security measures, we will explore the meticulous work being undertaken to ensure the Games' smooth operation. Technological advancements also play a crucial role, with the organizers implementing cutting-edge solutions to enhance communication, competition management, and the overall spectator experience.

Overview of paris 2024 preparation

As Paris gears up for the 33rd Olympic Games, the city is undergoing a major transformation that's set to reshape its urban fabric and facilities. The excitement begins on July 26 and concludes on August 11, 2024, marking the grandest event in France's history. It's a whirlwind of activity, with Paris tackling numerous projects to rejuvenate its iconic landscape. The Paris City Council is on a roll, greenlighting 43 initiatives aimed at fostering a greener, more vibrant, and accessible city for the upcoming Games. Plans include a bold "Swimming Plan" to make the Seine River suitable for Olympic water sports by installing new infrastructure to filter out bacteria and pollutants, showing Paris's commitment to a top-notch Olympic experience. Yet, amid the buzz of preparation, some folks are skeptical about Paris's ability to host the Games without a hitch. Despite Olympic organizers and French officials brimming with confidence, there's chatter about whether all the ambitious plans, especially the pricey cleanup of the Seine, can be realized in time. The city's public transportation system's ability to cope with the expected surge of visitors is another point of concern.Security is another hot topic, with plans to strengthen the regional police force for the Olympics. But even here, there's some tension, with police unions voicing their worries about working conditions and the clarity of security strategies. Despite these hurdles, progress is evident. Construction for new homes, stadiums, and venues is well on its way, with SOLIDEO, the construction oversight company, reporting that 84% of the work is done, on schedule and within budget. Yet, the readiness of Paris's public transport to manage the influx of fans remains questionable. Mayor Anne Hidalgo has flagged potential transport issues and overcrowding, prompting the city to develop navigation apps and alternative transit solutions for visitors. As the countdown to the Paris 2024 Olympics continues, Paris is all-in on hosting an epic event that captures the essence of sportsmanship, unity, and excellence. With a fusion of grit, ingenuity, and teamwork, Paris is set to flaunt the crème de la crème of French culture, hospitality, and athletic prowess on the global front.

Mascot

Mascot-wise, the 2024 Paris Olympics is taking a fresh and meaningful path with the Phryges. These aren't your typical animal or fantasy creatures; they're two red figures inspired by the Phrygian cap, a historic emblem of French liberty. The Phryges are more than just mascots; they're a nod to the Olympic spirit and French values. They're named after the cap that symbolized freedom in the French Revolution, and they stand for the enduring principles of liberty, equality, and brotherhood.

Each Phryge has a unique vibe. The Olympic Phryge radiates the enduring Olympic spirit, while the Paralympic Phryge, with its prosthetic running blade, celebrates diversity and the achievements of all athletes. These mascots, with their lively expressions and poses, are set to win hearts and energize crowds. They're not just for show; they're a vibrant part of the Olympic festivities, bringing joy wherever they go. But the Phryges are more than just fun figures. They embody unity, breaking down cultural barriers and bringing people together through the universal language of sportsmanship and the quest for greatness. They remind us that the Olympics are about more than just competition; they're about human potential, respect, and understanding across the globe.

The Phryges have become a staple in Paris, popping up on merchandise, at community events, and in educational programs, constantly reminding us of the Olympic ideals. As the Paris 2024 Olympics approach, the Phryges are more than mere mascots. They're symbols of freedom, inclusivity, and the life-changing impact of sports. They represent the heart of France and the Olympic spirit, celebrating our collective pursuit of excellence and the joy of the human spirit on an international stage.

Progress on infrastructure projects

France is gearing up to host a spectacular Olympic spectacle in 2024, with expectations to draw in over 10 million fans, and they're nearly ready, thanks to most of the necessary buildings and venues being good to go. This head start comes from Paris already having a bunch of top-notch facilities on hand when it scored the hosting gig back in 2017. The French are all hands on deck, getting everything set for the influx of global visitors. They're marking their calendars for July 26, the big kick-off, and they're confident that everything will be in tip-top shape for this massive celebration, building on what's already there.

Paris had a leg up when it came to getting ready for the Olympics because it already had a lot of what it needed when the city won the bid in 2017. Nicolas Ferrand, the big boss at Solideo, the crew in charge of getting the venues and infrastructure across the finish line, says they've knocked out 84% of the work, which is just a smidge behind the 89% they were shooting for. Still, they've made some serious progress and are well on their way to being ready.

Sure, they've hit a few bumps along the road, like figuring out security and dealing with some construction hiccups, but the vibe is still pretty positive about how things are shaping up. A few projects, like sprucing up the Grand Palais, getting the Olympic Village buildings squared away, and fixing up the Colombes swimming pool, are dragging a bit, but it's nothing they can't handle, and it shouldn't throw a wrench in the works for the competitions. One of the big wins was throwing open the doors to the La Chapelle sports center on July 11, up in the north part of town. This spot, which was part of the original Olympic plan, is ready to welcome 8,000 fans for some badminton and rhythmic gymnastics action. Plus, they're right on track with the stadium that'll later become the home court for Paris's basketball squad. They're also getting down to business on the Olympic Village, a huge 51-hectare patch in the capital's north that'll be home sweet home for 14,500 athletes during the games. The construction crew is a tad behind on the athlete housing, but they're hustling to catch up and make sure everything's good to go.

Another big deal is that they've finished the Aquatic Centre, a shiny new spot made just for the Olympics, sitting right across from the Stade de France. This is where the synchronized swimming and diving will go down, while other swimming showdowns will happen at the spruced-up Defence Arena to the northwest.

Even with a few curveballs and delays, Paris is all in on making sure the 2024 Olympics are one for the history books. The city's got big dreams for a more inclusive and green future, and the Olympics are speeding that up, getting props from all over for how the games can transform a city and get the community jazzed.

Now, about the Seine River—it's smack dab in the middle of Paris and it's both a super cool opportunity and a bit of a puzzle for the 2024 Olympics. The city's got big plans to use the river for the opening ceremony and some swimming events, but they've got to make sure the water's clean enough first.

The Seine's set to be a star of the show, with the opening ceremony and open water swimming ready to make a splash. But getting the river ready for its close-up has been a bit tricky, with heavy rain and keeping the water clean enough for everyone. Enter the Austerlitz storage basin, this huge project that's all about keeping the Seine in tip-top shape, especially when it pours. This massive rainwater tank is no joke—it's going to hold up to 46 million liters of rainwater, which helps keep pollution at bay.

With the Austerlitz basin done, Paris is one step closer to making sure the Seine is ready for its Olympic moment. Once it's up and running, this basin is going to be a key player in keeping the river's water quality in check, which is super important for the health of the athletes and everyone coming to watch. But that's not all—Paris has been busy with all sorts of projects to cut down on pollution and make the Seine healthier. They're beefing up the sewerage network, keeping a close eye on the water, and doing all sorts of tests to make sure the Olympic experience is not just fun, but safe and green too.

Even with Mother Nature throwing some curveballs, Paris isn't backing down. They're determined to turn the Seine into an unforgettable venue for the Olympic festivities. With some smart thinking and teamwork, they're getting ready to show off the Seine's charm and make sure the Olympic experience on the water is nothing short of amazing.

Sustainability initiatives planned for the Games

The upcoming Paris 2024 Olympic and Paralympic Games are gearing up to break new ground in how big sporting events handle environmental care. They've got a game plan that's not just about wowing the world and welcoming everyone, but also about being super mindful of our planet. The team behind the scenes is shaking things up to change what we expect from the Olympics.

At the core of their game plan for a greener Olympics is a promise to slash their carbon footprint in half compared to past Games. They're aiming for under 1.7 million tons of CO_2 before the starting whistle even blows. This huge goal is making them rethink everything with a green lens. When it comes to where the magic happens, 95% of the spots for the Paris 2024 showdown are going to be places that already exist or pop-up spots that'll be taken down later. This is a big win for the planet, showing how we can make sports events eco-friendly from the ground up.

For the new spots they are building, like the swimming hub and the home base for athletes, they're sticking to tough eco-friendly rules. They're picking materials and building methods that are kind to the climate, showing off their dedication to a smaller carbon footprint. Paris 2024 is also leading the charge with clean energy, powering places like the athletes' village with the heat from the earth and the sun's rays. They're hooking up with wind and solar farms too, cutting down emissions and setting the stage for a future where clean energy is the norm.

They're also on a mission to make getting around greener. They've picked venues easy to get to by public transport and are giving bike lanes a boost. Fans will have loads of public transport options, including rides powered by electricity and hydrogen from Toyota, helping everyone move around without dirtying the air. But wait, there's more. Paris 2024's eco-friendly moves are making waves way beyond the Games. They're working with big names like the OECD to come up with new ways to see how events impact our world. They're even helping to update international standards, showing they're serious about a greener, more sustainable world for us all.

Paris 2024 is really changing the game when it comes to hosting the Olympics. They're all about being eco-smart, super creative, and including everyone. With their bold steps and game-changing plans, they're hoping to leave a green legacy that'll inspire us to think about our planet in everything we do.

Security measures and contingency planning

The security framework established for the 2024 Paris Olympics is exceptionally robust, particularly concerning the inaugural festivities along the Seine. Recent disturbances within France have heightened public apprehension, prompting event organizers to implement comprehensive measures to ensure stringent security. Envision the transformation of the Seine into a grand stage, presenting a formidable security endeavor. An impressive deployment of 35,000 law enforcement officers, complemented by an extensive contingent of private security personnel, will be dedicated to maintaining order and safeguarding attendees.

Consider the deployment of advanced surveillance technology: an additional 400 state-of-the-art cameras will augment the 4,000 already operational throughout Paris. These sophisticated devices are equipped to detect any anomalies, such as unattended items or overcrowding.

Moreover, contingency strategies are meticulously devised to address any potential emergencies. These plans consider all logistical aspects, including accommodation and transportation, to prevent any disruptions to the event's smooth execution. Preparatory exercises are being conducted along the river, alongside demonstrations of innovative aerial defense systems designed to neutralize intrusive drones. The objective is to remain proactive in all security aspects.

In summary, an all-encompassing effort is being made to ensure that the opening celebration of the Paris 2024 Olympics is not only memorable but also exceptionally secure. This complex endeavor involves numerous dynamic elements, yet the dedicated team is fully committed to providing a secure and enjoyable experience for all participants.

All About the Sports

New sports debuting in Paris 2024

The Olympic Games constantly transform, mirroring the fluidity of sports and the varied interests of participants and viewers alike. With the approach of the Paris 2024 Olympics, the excitement builds for the debut of new, captivating sports and disciplines that are set to enthrall a global audience. The high-energy performances of breakdancing, the ascending trials of sport climbing, the thrilling rides of surfing, and the awe-inspiring maneuvers of skateboarding signal the advent of a fresh chapter in athletic prowess and creativity.

Moreover, the Olympic program's expansion to include kiteboarding under the sailing category broadens the scope of aquatic competitions, underscoring the ingenuity and versatility of water sports on an international platform. Yet, as we welcome these novel events, we must also acknowledge the absence of sports such as karate, baseball, and softball, underlining the constantly evolving roster of Olympic disciplines. As we navigate the evolving sports terrain of Paris 2024, we encourage you to delve into the rich tapestry of disciplines, the narratives of determination and resilience, and the persistent ethos of excellence that epitomize the Olympic Games. We invite you to join in the celebration of the athletes, the diverse sports, and the unifying spirit of competition that binds us in the collective quest for glory.

Breakdancing

Breakdancing is set to create a historic moment at the Paris 2024 Olympic Games, where for the first time, B-boys and B-girls will vie for Olympic medals, representing a significant evolution for a discipline that originated in the Bronx's urban landscape. Emerging from the New York City streets in the 1970s, breakdancing has consistently been marked by its originality and artistic flair. Breakers, the athletes of this sport, have continually expanded the frontiers of physical artistry and self-expression. In 2024, these athletes will break new ground as they become the highlight of the Olympics, making breakdancing the inaugural dance sport to grace this prestigious event.

The International Olympic Committee's (IOC) decision to incorporate breakdancing signifies a shift away from its conventional focus on sports with established club systems. Breaking's inclusion highlights its organic, community-driven essence, with informal crews engaging in competitive dance battles. As the breakdancing community eagerly awaits its Olympic debut, some members express concerns. They worry about how the impromptu and artistic spirit of breaking will align with the structured nature of competitive sports. Thorsten Süfke, President of the Berlin Dance Sport Association, points out the nuanced task of maintaining breaking's cultural ethos within the Olympic setting.

Nonetheless, the proposed format for the 2024 Olympic breakdancing events is designed to honor the individual artistry and flair of the competitors. In head-to-head solo battles, 16 male and 16 female dancers will compete, aiming to win over the judges with their distinctive moves and prowess. The judging criteria are set to encompass aspects like originality, personality, technical skill, adaptability, performance quality, and rhythmic interpretation to truly reflect the spirit of breaking while promoting fairness and impartiality.

The breakdancing events are scheduled for August 9 and 10, featuring both the women's and men's categories, with qualifying rounds and finals. Spectators can look forward to a weekend brimming with dynamic performances and awe-inspiring routines as the finest breakers from across the globe pursue Olympic success.

Notable figures in the breakdancing world, such as Phil Wizard from Canada and Shigekix from Japan in the men's bracket, and Logistx from the US and Ami from Japan in the women's bracket, are poised to excel at the Olympics. These exceptional dancers, among others, will demonstrate the physicality, artistry, and essence of breakdancing on this international platform, securing its reputation as a distinguished global sport.

Sports climbing

Sport climbing, following its triumphant inaugural showing at the Tokyo 2020 Olympics, is poised for its encore at the Paris 2024 Games. This contemporary sport will be showcased at the Le Bourget Sport Climbing Venue located in Saint-Denis, where the number of athletes participating will increase to a total of 68. The competition structure will differ from that of Tokyo 2020, where competitors vied across all three disciplines (speed, bouldering, and lead) to earn a single 'combined' medal. In contrast, the Paris 2024 Olympics will introduce a revised format featuring two distinct medal events.

Here's a breakdown of the discipline and format for sport climbing at the 2024 Olympics:

Discipline breakdown:

Speed: In this exciting climbing challenge, a pair of competitors scale a fixed 15-meter path set at a slight five-degree angle. The aim is simple: get to the summit faster than anyone else. Guys often conquer the route in less than six seconds, and the ladies strive to beat the seven-second mark.

Bouldering: Competitors in this event strive to scale four distinct challenges, each referred to as a "problem," with the goal being to conquer the summit with the least number of tries. Every challenge is segmented into three areas, and participants rack up points by touching each area with both hands.

Lead: Scaling an uncharted path, climbers have a six-minute window to reach the top. They've got to secure their rope to every quickdraw on the way up. Come Paris 2024, there'll be two sets of medals up for grabs for each gender in climbing: one for Speed and another for the Combined event, which includes both Boulder and Lead challenges.

Speed event:

The Speed event is set to be a thrilling showdown, with expert climbers racing against each other. We've got 28 contenders—14 men and 14 women—lined up, and they'll all go through a qualifying round to see who makes it to the final cut. Mark your calendars for the 7th and 8th of August, 2024, because that's when the top qualifiers will battle it out for the prestigious title and the very first individual Olympic gold in the realm of speed climbing. Keep an eye out for stars like Italy's Matteo Zurloni and Poland's Aleksandra Miroslaw, who've already clinched their spots for this epic event.

Combined event:

The Combined event will feature competitors vying for the top prize in both the bouldering and lead climbing categories. Participants have the opportunity to accumulate up to 200 points in total, with each category offering a potential 100 points.

In the bouldering category, contestants score points by successfully navigating to specific zones and completing each climbing problem. In lead climbing, the scoring is contingent upon the climber's ability to ascend to the furthest hold.

The contender who amasses the greatest combined score will earn the prestigious title of Combined Olympic Champion. Toby Roberts is poised to enter the annals of history as the inaugural male representative for Team GB in sport climbing at the Olympic Games, following his victory at the combined European Qualifiers. The sport climbing events at the Paris 2024 Olympics are anticipated to be a spectacle of physical skill, tactical acumen, and creative flair. The competition will not only be a quest for Olympic medals but also serve as an inspiration for the next wave of athletes to aim high and pursue their dreams.

Surfing

Surfing is poised for a spectacular reemergence at the Paris 2024 Olympics, with the iconic waves of French Polynesia's Teahupo'o set to host the event. This choice spotlights a captivating display of skill, as competitors will engage with some of the planet's most formidable waves, a stark contrast to Paris's metropolitan setting.

Teahupo'o is celebrated for its towering surf and challenging breaks, making it an apt stage for the Olympics. Its waves, known for their size and power, pose a significant test for even the most experienced surfers. The locale's name, which in Tahitian means "wall of heads," speaks to the intensity of the surf, mirroring the area's storied past.

Hosting the Olympic surfing competition in such a distant locale has sparked discussions regarding the logistical and environmental impacts. With Paris committed to a low-carbon Olympic footprint, transporting participants and audiences to French Polynesia has raised sustainability questions. Yet, for aficionados, the magnetic pull of Teahupo'o's legendary waves is irresistible. The promise of witnessing top-tier surfers navigate these formidable waters fuels enthusiasm for the upcoming Games.

Athletes will earn their spots at Paris 2024 through a series of demanding events under the governance of the International Surfing Association (ISA) and the World Surf League (WSL). With an equal number of 24 male and 24 female surfers competing, the event is sure to be highly competitive. These athletes will demonstrate their prowess and daring as they contend with the perilous Teahupo'o surf, aiming to secure their place in representing their nations. Despite the logistical hurdles of its secluded setting, Teahupo'o encapsulates the essence of surfing—a sport deeply rooted in nature, celebrating physical excellence, bravery, and fellowship. As the surfing world gears up for the Paris 2024 Olympics in French Polynesia, the stage is set for what is anticipated to be a memorable chapter in Olympic history.

Skateboarding

The 2024 Paris Olympics is poised to once again capture the attention of spectators with the inclusion of skateboarding, where elite athletes will demonstrate their prowess in the thrilling categories of street and park. Anticipate high-energy performances on Saturday, July 27, and Sunday, July 28, for street skateboarding, while the park competition will command the spotlight on Tuesday, August 6, and Wednesday, August 7. Set against the historic backdrop of Place de La Concorde, the skateboarding events will unfold, complementing the Parisian scenery with the vigor of modern sportsmanship. This venue will also host other urban sports, including BMX freestyle and 3x3 basketball, fostering a vibrant celebration of contemporary youth culture and ingenuity. Competitors in the street category will tackle a course simulating a cityscape, complete with ramps, rails, and various urban challenges. The park category will see skateboarders navigating a landscape of bowls and pools, emphasizing their inventive flair and dexterity.

The Paris 2024 Olympics introduces a revamped scoring system for skateboarding that strives for fairness between the two segments of the event: runs and tricks. Each athlete will execute two 45-second runs and a series of tricks. In contrast to the previous methodology where only the top four scores were considered, the new system assigns scores ranging from 0 to 100. An athlete's highest-scoring run and their two top tricks will be aggregated for their overall score, balancing the importance of both event segments. Moreover, the newly implemented Scoring Refusal Procedure grants competitors the option to discard a trick attempt without facing penalties, thus offering them a strategic advantage to enhance their overall performance. With these innovative modifications and a roster of skilled participants, the skateboarding contests at the upcoming Paris Olympics are set to deliver a spectacle of skill, exhilaration, and memorable instances that embody the energetic essence of this esteemed athletic discipline.

Brief explanations and rules of each sport

Archery

Archery is among the most ancient sports practiced by humans, evolving with civilization itself, initially for hunting and combat. Its origins can be traced to 1200 BC, with civilizations such as the Hittites and Assyrians employing archery in warfare. Organized archery competitions began in ancient China during the Zhou dynasty (1027-256 BC). The sport's international growth was later overseen by the International Archery Federation, now called World Archery, founded in 1931. The sport of archery demands precision and focus. Archers strive to hit a target with a 122cm diameter from a distance of 70m, aiming for the center—a challenge that requires extraordinary concentration and skill. Olympic archery includes five events: individual and team events for both men and women, plus a mixed team event that debuted at the Tokyo 2020 Olympics.

Archery competitions proceed through elimination rounds after a ranking round where each archer shoots 72 arrows. Competitors face off in one-on-one matches determined by their rankings, with the highest-ranked archer competing against the 64th, the second against the 63rd, and so on. Archery has had two periods of Olympic presence. It premiered at the 1900 Paris Olympics and was featured again in 1904, 1908, and 1920. Following a lengthy absence, it was reintroduced at the 1972 Munich Olympics and has been a consistent presence ever since. Since its Olympic return, the Republic of Korea has been a dominant force, clinching over half the gold medals, with 27 out of 45. The archery events at the 2024 Paris Olympics are scheduled from July 25th to August 4th at the Invalides. The Esplanade des Invalides, located in Paris' 7th arrondissement and facing the majestic Hôtel des Invalides, offers a venue that blends history, culture, and sporting excellence, providing an iconic stage for the world's premier archers to vie for Olympic medals.

Athletics

Track and field, with origins dating to the first Olympic Games in 776 BC, is recognized as the most ancient sport with a history of recorded champions from bygone eras. Originally, it included foot races and a pentathlon composed of running, jumping, discus, javelin, and wrestling. Over time, track and field has become a fundamental aspect of the contemporary Olympic tradition. Today's track and field maintains its variety, with events that include running, jumping, throwing, walking, and multi-sport competitions, making it the sport with the highest level of participation in the Olympics. The track events consist of short sprints to long-distance runs, hurdles, steeplechases, and relay races, all taking place on the standard 400m track within the Olympic venue. The marathon and race walking, which require both stamina and strategic skill, are held on city streets.

The sport features two multi-discipline events: the heptathlon for women and the decathlon for men, which unfold over two days and challenge competitors in a range of track and field events. These contests occur in the Olympic stadium, utilizing specialized areas for jumping and throwing, as athletes compete to secure their spots in the final rounds.

Track and field has been a pivotal part of the Olympics since the first modern games in Athens in 1896, and its importance has only increased. Women's competitions were added in 1928 and have gradually evolved to provide an equal number of events for both genders. The 1960s saw an explosion in global participation in track and field, culminating in a multicultural assembly of competitors at the 2008 Beijing Olympics.

For the upcoming Paris 2024 Olympics, track and field events are slated to take place from August 1st to August 11th. The schedule includes a diverse mix of disciplines, from rapid sprints to enduring marathons, obstacle races, relay teams, jumps, throws, and combined events. This extensive agenda promises a captivating showcase of skill and resilience, solidifying track and field's eminent position as the pinnacle event of the summer Games.

Badminton

Badminton, which evolved from the ancient game of Battledor and Shuttlecock, has developed into a globally recognized competitive sport with a rich history. Its transformation into the modern game is not fully understood, but it is believed to have begun at the Badminton House estate in Gloucestershire, owned by the Duke of Beaufort, which is also the sport's namesake. Badminton spread from Europe to India, throughout the British colonies, and into East Asia, where it has become a favored sport internationally. The game is played at a brisk pace, with either individual players or pairs competing indoors. Participants use a shuttlecock and aim to land it within the opponent's court or force an error. A match is won by securing two out of three games, each game being played to 21 points.

Badminton was first showcased at the 1972 Munich Olympics as a demonstration sport. It became an exhibition sport in Seoul in 1988, and was officially included in the Olympic program starting with the 1992 Barcelona Games. The sport initially featured singles and doubles events for both men and women, with mixed doubles introduced at the Atlanta 1996 Games. Asian countries have been particularly successful in Olympic badminton, often leading the medal count. At the upcoming Paris 2024 Olympics, 172 athletes will vie for medals over five events: men's singles, women's singles, men's doubles, women's doubles, and mixed doubles. The competitions will span ten days, culminating in the presentation of medals. The Porte de la Chapelle Arena in Paris, a contemporary venue designed for sporting events and performances, will host the badminton events from July 27th to August 5th. The arena's sustainable design and lasting legacy post-Games make it an ideal venue for showcasing the dynamic nature of Olympic badminton.

Basketball

Basketball, created by James W. Naismith in 1891 as a way to keep students physically active during winter, has maintained many of its foundational rules through to the present day. The sport quickly gained traction and led to international competitions in the 1920s, with the first World Championships for men and women being held in the 1950s. Played by two teams of five on a rectangular court, the objective in basketball is to score by propelling the ball through a hoop elevated 3.05 meters above the ground. Olympic basketball consists of four quarters, each lasting 10 minutes, where players exhibit stamina, agility, and skill. Basketball appeared as a demonstration sport at 1904 St. Louis Games and became an official Olympic sport at the 1936 Berlin Games.

Women's basketball was added to the Olympics in 1976 in Montreal. Historically, the United States has dominated Olympic basketball, with both men's and women's teams achieving numerous victories. The Paris 2024 Olympics will feature basketball competitions from July 27th to August 10th at the renowned Bercy Arena. Known for its pyramid design, the Bercy Arena has been a Parisian cultural and sporting landmark since 1984 and is poised to host the basketball tournament after recent renovations.

3x3 Basketball

3x3 basketball, recognized as a leading urban sport, has its roots in street basketball's informal and inventive settings. The International Basketball Federation (FIBA), which also oversees traditional 5x5 basketball, has fostered the growth of 3x3 basketball, as seen in events like the 3x3 World Tour and France's 3x3 Superleague, known for their vibrant atmospheres and musical entertainment. This version is played on a half-court with teams of three, featuring a single hoop and a blend of offensive and defensive play. The game is quick, with a 10-minute duration or until a team scores 21 points.

The two-point line adds a strategic element to the scoring process. 3x3 basketball debuted at the 2010 Youth Olympic Games in Singapore and was included in the Tokyo 2020 Games by the IOC, highlighting its growing appeal. The 3x3 basketball events at Paris 2024 will captivate audiences from July 30th to August 5th at the Place de la Concorde, an iconic location that will merge urban sports with the city's historic grandeur for a memorable Olympic experience.

Boxing

Boxing, an ancient combat sport, dates back to the 3rd millennium BCE, with origins in civilizations such as Sumer. It became part of the ancient Olympic Games in 688 BC and resurfaced as a sport in 17th-century England, with the first records of amateur boxing dating from 1880. Olympic boxing, which traditionally featured amateur competitors until the Rio 2016 Games, now also allows professional boxers to qualify. Judges score each round based on performance, determining the winner.

Boxing has been a consistent feature of the Summer Olympics since its debut in 1904, with the exception of the 1912 Games. Women's boxing was added in 2012. The United States, Cuba, and Great Britain are the leading nations in Olympic boxing medals. The boxing events at Paris 2024 will take place from July 27th to August 10th, with preliminary rounds hosted at the North Paris Arena in the Villepinte exhibition center, a venue significant for both Olympic and Paralympic events.

Canoe Slalom

Canoe slalom, a thrilling aquatic sport, stems from the traditional use of kayaks by Eskimos and the historical use of canoes for transport and trade. Competitive canoeing emerged in the mid-19th century, with the London Royal Canoe Club playing a key role in the sport's development. Olympic canoe slalom, alongside canoe sprint, requires athletes to navigate a course with up to 25 gates, where penalties are given for gate infractions. Competitors use either kayaks or canoes, with different paddling techniques for each. The sport made its Olympic debut in 1972 and became a permanent event in 1992. European athletes have won the majority of Olympic canoe slalom medals. Paris 2024 will introduce a new kayak cross event, adding to the sport's excitement. The canoe slalom competitions at the Paris 2024 Olympics will occur from July 27th to August 5th at the Vaires-sur-Marne Nautical Stadium, a modern facility inaugurated in 2019, ready to host Olympic canoe-kayak and rowing events.

Canoe sprint

Canoe sprinting emerged from the traditional use of canoes for travel and hunting in diverse areas such as North America, Siberia, and Greenland, eventually evolving into a competitive sport by the middle of the 19th century, especially in Great Britain. The establishment of the London Royal Canoe Club in 1866 was pivotal in shaping the sport.

In the discipline of canoe sprint, competitors race on flatwater courses that are straight and span distances of 200m, 500m, and 1000m. These races, which are conducted in lanes similar to those in rowing competitions, involve eight lanes per race. The goal is straightforward: to be the first to reach the finish line. There are a variety of canoe sprint categories, including individual events such as the canoe single (C1) and kayak single (K1), pair events like the canoe double (C2) and kayak double (K2), and team events with four members (kayak four – K4). The sport of canoe sprint was officially included in the Olympic Games in Berlin in 1936, after being showcased at the Paris Games in 1924. Women's participation in kayak events at the Olympics began with the 1948 London Games.

The canoe sprint competitions at the 2024 Paris Olympics are scheduled to take place from August 6th to August 10th at the Vaires-sur-Marne Nautical Stadium. Opened in June 2019, this venue in Seine-et-Marne (77) boasts modern facilities designed to accommodate both Olympic and Paralympic canoe-kayak and rowing competitions, providing an ideal environment for athletes to display their speed and skill in the quest for Olympic medals.

Road cycling

Road cycling dates back to the advent of the bicycle in the 19th century and quickly became a favored recreational activity. This led to the organization of races by the end of that century. National cycling bodies were formed, and in 1900, the International Cycling Union (Union Cycliste Internationale) was established to oversee cycling disciplines globally. At the Olympics, road cycling features two primary events: the mass-start road race and the individual time trial. The road race covers over 120km for women and over 200km for men, often culminating in a strategic sprint finish. In contrast, the individual time trial is a race against the clock over distances generally shorter than 50km, focusing on consistent pacing and aerodynamics.

Road cycling has been an Olympic event since the inaugural modern Games in 1896, although it was not included in a few editions. The program has expanded to include women's cycling since 1984 and the time trial since 1996. During the 2024 Paris Olympics, the time trial events are set for July 27th, with the road races following on August 3rd for men and August 4th for women. The courses will pass by Parisian landmarks such as the Trocadéro and the Esplanade des Invalides, offering spectators a close view of the action. The men's road race will extend for 273 km, with a final ascent on the Butte Montmartre, while the women's race will be 158 km long with its own significant climb. Both races will begin and end at the Trocadéro. The time trial will lead athletes from Les Invalides to the Bois de Vincennes and back, finishing at the Pont Alexandre III.

Track cycling

Originating in England in the 1870s, track cycling began with the construction of indoor wooden tracks. It gained widespread popularity, leading to the first World Championships in Chicago in 1893. Track cycling takes place in a velodrome, a 250-meter oval track, with cyclists riding brakeless, fixed-gear bikes. Track cycling includes a variety of race formats, each with distinctive rules and strategic demands. For instance, the individual sprint is different in approach from the 25km omnium race.

Since its introduction to the Olympic Games in 1896, with the exception of the 1912 Stockholm Games, track cycling has been a mainstay. Women's events were added at the 1988 Seoul Olympics. Historically, European nations such as the UK, France, the Netherlands, and Italy have excelled, but countries like Australia are increasingly competitive. The 2024 Paris Olympics will feature track cycling events like the Team Sprint, Sprint, Keirin, Team Pursuit, Omnium, and Madison at the National Velodrome from August 5th to August 11th. The National Velodrome, designed for premier competitions, will serve as a cutting-edge arena for the world's elite track cyclists to vie for Olympic success.

BMX freestyle

BMX freestyle, which sprang from the Californian racing scene of the 1970s, traces its lineage to the inventive spirits of youthful riders captivated by the stunts of their predecessors. As time progressed, the sport's appeal surged, leading to its inclusion in prominent extreme sports events like the X Games and the FISE International Festival of Extreme Sports. The UCI launched the inaugural BMX Freestyle World Cup in 2016 under the FISE umbrella. Competitors in BMX freestyle contests execute stunts in urban parks, striving to demonstrate their prowess, originality, and flair in routines lasting 60 seconds. Panels of judges evaluate these performances, considering the complexity of the stunts, the amplitude of the jumps, and the finesse of the execution.

BMX freestyle first graced the Olympic platform at the 2018 Youth Olympic Games in Buenos Aires, garnering accolades from spectators and the IOC. It was then embraced for the Tokyo 2020 Games, infusing the cycling disciplines with a dynamic and exhilarating dimension. The BMX freestyle competitions at the Paris 2024 Olympics are scheduled for July 30th and 31st at the La Concorde Urban Park, a venue that melds the thrill of modern sports with a historically rich Parisian setting. The UCI is the global authority responsible for the stewardship and regulatory oversight of BMX freestyle, ensuring the sport's continued growth and integrity worldwide.

BMX racing

BMX racing, which took inspiration from the 1960s motocross fever in California, saw children imitating their two-wheeled heroes. By the early 1980s, BMX had matured into an established sport with its own federation, and the first BMX World Championships were held in 1982. The UCI adopted BMX as a discipline in 1993, setting the stage for its Olympic debut. In BMX racing, competitors engage in swift sprints on tracks replete with jumps, banked turns, and various challenges. With up to eight riders per race, the sport is known for its intense, short-duration energy demands. Riders burst from an 8-meter-high starting hill onto a 400-meter course, reaching speeds that can exceed 60 km/h. Quick reflexes and powerful starts are key to gaining the lead and securing victory.

BMX racing was introduced as a full medal sport at the Beijing 2008 Olympics after the IOC's endorsement in 2003. Although it has a brief Olympic tenure, athletes like Mariana Pajón of Colombia and Niek Kimmann of the Netherlands have become notable figures, with high expectations for their performance in the Paris 2024 Games. The BMX racing events at the Paris 2024 Olympics will unfold on August 1st and 2nd at the Saint-Quentin-en-Yvelines BMX Stadium, a specialized facility within the National Velodrome that allows BMX racing and track cycling to be enjoyed concurrently by fans.

Equestrian

Equestrianism boasts an ancient lineage, with origins in Greece where it served as combat training. Although it experienced a period of decline, the Renaissance saw its revival. Today's Olympic equestrian events encompass three disciplines: jumping, dressage, and eventing, where men and women compete equally.

- Jumping challenges riders and horses to clear a course of obstacles within a set time, minimizing penalties.
- Dressage pairs horse and rider in a choreographed display to music, emphasizing grace and unity.
- Eventing tests the all-around abilities of horse and rider through a combination of the previous disciplines, including a cross-country segment.

Equestrian sports officially entered the Olympic program in Stockholm in 1912. By 1964, all equestrian events were open to female competitors, making it a uniquely mixed discipline in the Olympics, with individual and team medals awarded. The Paris 2024 Olympics will feature equestrian events from July 27th to August 6th against the stunning backdrop of the Château de Versailles, promising a memorable spectacle for attendees.

Fencing

Fencing's heritage spans millennia, progressing from ancient swordplay to a refined sport under the tutelage of European masters. It is now a global activity with 157 national federations under the International Fencing Federation. Fencers duel with one of three weapons—foil, épée, or sabre—and aim to land strikes on specific target areas. The foil and épée require point contact, while the sabre allows for scoring with the blade's edge or back. Victory is achieved by reaching a predetermined point total or having the highest score when time expires.

Since its inclusion in the first modern Olympics in 1896, with women's events added in 1924, fencing has been a staple of the Games. One of the sport's legends is Nedo Nadi of Italy, who won gold in all three weapons at the 1920 Games. The Paris 2024 Olympics will host fencing events from July 27th to August 4th at the Grand Palais, an architectural marvel that will enhance the elegance and athleticism of the world's elite fencers.

Soccer

Soccer, with roots in ancient China and modern developments in England, has become the most beloved sport globally. It has been an Olympic fixture since the 1900 Paris Games, with memorable performances from icons like Ferenc Puskás, Lionel Messi, and Marta. The 2024 Paris Olympics will again feature soccer, with men's and women's tournaments adhering to FIFA rules on grass pitches. The Parc des Princes and Stade de la Beaujoire are among the storied venues hosting the matches.

These tournaments not only display premier athletic talent but also foster unity and fair play, embodying the Olympic ethos. As supporters from around the globe converge, Olympic football continues to be a symbol of international camaraderie and shared passion.

Golf

Golf, with its historical roots stretching to the 15th-century Netherlands and officially codified in 1754 at St Andrews, Scotland, has developed into an internationally celebrated sport with a following of millions. Since the advent of women's competitions in the late 19th century, the game has captivated a global audience, now boasting upwards of 60 million participants and over 30,000 courses. In this sport, competitors strive to traverse an 18-hole course, employing a variety of clubs to propel the ball into each hole using the least number of strokes. At the Olympic level, the sport is contested in a stroke play format, with athletes completing the course four times across four days. The player with the lowest total score at the conclusion of the competition is declared the winner.

Golf made a triumphant Olympic return at the 2016 Rio Games and continued its presence in Tokyo 2020. It will be featured once more at the 2024 Paris Olympics, with events scheduled from August 1st to 10th.

Le Golf National, a course with a legacy of hosting premier events like the French Open and the Ryder Cup since 1991, will host the Olympic golf events. Competitors will vie for victory against the picturesque setting of Le Golf National, where the ethos of competition and fellowship will be honored, all under the governance of the International Golf Federation.

Artistic gymnastics

Artistic gymnastics, with origins in antiquity and formally recognized as a competitive sport in 1881 through the founding of the International Gymnastics Federation, has been a cornerstone of the Olympic Games since their modern inception in Athens in 1896. Competitors in artistic gymnastics engage in both individual and team events on various apparatuses, demonstrating their strength, agility, coordination, and precision. The men's category includes the floor exercise, pommel horse, rings, vault, parallel bars, and horizontal bar, while the women's category comprises the vault, uneven bars, balance beam, and floor exercise.

The sport has seen periods of dominance by nations such as Japan, the Soviet Union, East Germany, the USA, Russia, and China. A significant scoring overhaul occurred in 2005, introducing a system that combines difficulty (D-score) and execution (E-score), replacing the prior 10-point maximum and allowing for more nuanced differentiation between performances. During the Paris 2024 Olympics, artistic gymnastics will captivate global audiences from July 27th to August 5th at the Bercy Arena. Known for its distinctive pyramid design, this venue has been a central location for cultural and sports events since 1984, epitomizing the blend of heritage and contemporary spirit in Paris' 12th arrondissement. Gymnasts from across the globe will gather at Bercy Arena to vie for Olympic medals and display their artistry.

Rhythmic gymnastics

Rhythmic gymnastics, a mesmerizing blend of dance and gymnastic elements, emerged as a separate discipline in the mid-20th century, growing out of the group gymnastics traditions in Europe. It gained official recognition from the International Gymnastics Federation (FIG) in 1961, and the first World Championships followed in Budapest in 1963. This exclusively female discipline features athletes performing with four types of apparatus – ribbon, hoop, ball, and clubs – to music that often includes vocals. Individual routines, lasting between 75 and 90 seconds, and group routines, with five gymnasts, are judged on difficulty, artistry, and execution.

Rhythmic gymnastics entered the Olympic program with individual events and expanded to include group events in Atlanta 1996. While Eastern European countries, especially Russia, have traditionally been strong contenders, nations such as Spain, Canada, and Israel have also challenged their dominance. The 2024 Paris Olympic rhythmic gymnastics events will enchant viewers from August 8th to 10th at the Porte de La Chapelle Arena. This modern venue, designed with sustainability in mind, serves as a cultural beacon in northern Paris and is set to leave a lasting legacy post-Games. Athletes will take to the floor to display the elegance and skill of rhythmic gymnastics to the world.

Trampolining

Trampolining, the brainchild of American gymnast George Nissen in 1934, was inspired by the aerial stunts of circus performers on safety nets. Initially intended to train astronauts and athletes, the trampoline quickly gained popularity as a competitive sport. London played host to the first Trampoline World Championships in 1964, and by 1998, the sport was incorporated into the International Gymnastics Federation.

Competitive trampolining features athletes reaching heights of over 8 meters, performing a series of complex maneuvers including twists, bounces, and flips, with each routine consisting of ten elements evaluated for difficulty, execution, and time spent airborne. Precision and technical skill are crucial in this high-flying sport. Since its Olympic debut at the Sydney 2000 Games, trampolining has been a part of the gymnastics disciplines, with both men's and women's individual events. China has been particularly successful, claiming a significant portion of the Olympic medals, including four golds. Notably, Canada's Rosie MacLennan has twice defended her Olympic title, in 2012 and 2016. The trampoline events at the 2024 Paris Olympics are set to excite audiences on August 2nd at the Bercy Arena, a venue celebrated for its unique pyramid shape in Paris' 12th arrondissement, providing an ideal backdrop for the dynamic performances of the trampolining athletes.

Handball

Handball, with roots tracing back to Scandinavia and Germany in the late 19th century, initially had two variants: outdoor and indoor handball. By 1966, indoor handball had become the prevalent form, evolving into the game we recognize today. The game is played on a 40m x 20m court, where two teams of seven players compete to score by hurling a ball into the opposing team's goal. Players are permitted to take three steps without bouncing the ball and can hold it for a maximum of three seconds. The team with the most goals after two halves, each lasting 30 minutes, is declared the winner.

Handball is a physical sport, allowing body contact between players, which demands stamina and strength. The sport prioritizes offensive play, discouraging inactivity. Competitors require endurance, power, strategic understanding, cooperation, and adaptability, as they switch between attack and defense. Outdoor handball was introduced in the 1936 Berlin Olympics and appeared as a demonstration sport in the 1952 Helsinki Games. Indoor handball was included in the Munich 1972 Olympics, with the women's event added in Montreal 1976. European countries have largely dominated the sport, with

South Korea as a notable exception, securing medals in the 1988 Seoul and 1992 Barcelona Games. For the 2024 Paris Olympics, the handball tournaments for men and women will occur from July 25th to August 11th. The Paris Sud 6 Arena will host the qualification matches, while the Pierre Mauroy Stadium in Lille will stage the final rounds. This modern multi-use stadium, established in 2012, is set to provide an excellent venue for the thrilling handball competitions.

Hockey

Hockey, originating from the French term "hocquet," has a history spanning millennia, with early versions found in various ancient civilizations. The sport, as we know it, crystallized in England during the mid-19th century, with formal rules codified in 1876. Characterized by its pace, skill, and excitement, hockey games consist of 60 minutes, divided into four 15-minute quarters. Teams field eleven players, including forwards, midfielders, defenders, and a goalkeeper, with the option for limitless substitutions. Using curved sticks, players aim to score by hitting a hard ball into the opponent's goal, with only the flat side of the stick allowed for striking the ball.

Hockey made its Olympic debut in the 1908 London Games and has been a regular feature since 1928, with the women's competition introduced in 1980. While traditionally dominated by Anglo-Saxon nations such as India, Pakistan, Australia, and Great Britain, the sport has achieved a global spread, with countries like Argentina, the Netherlands, Germany, Belgium, Spain, and France emerging as strong contenders. At the Tokyo Olympics, Belgium and the Netherlands secured gold in the men's and women's categories, respectively. The Paris 2024 hockey events, scheduled from July 27th to August 9th, will be held at the historic Yves du Manoir Stadium, which also hosted the 1924 Olympics, making it a significant site for the sport. Hockey continues to engage audiences internationally, upholding the Olympic values of teamwork, proficiency, and fair play.

Judo

Judo, or "the gentle way" in Japanese, is a martial art established by Dr. Jigoro Kano in 1882. It evolved from jujitsu, with Kano's intention to preserve its essential techniques while removing more hazardous elements. Judo was the first martial art to gain significant traction outside Japan, especially in Europe during the late 20th century. In judo, competitors aim to throw their opponent to the mat, secure them with a pin, or compel a submission through joint locks or chokes. Victories are achieved through Ippon (a full-point score from a decisive throw or submission) or by accumulating two Waza-ari (half-point scores). Penalties may be imposed for passive conduct or actions against judo's ethos.

Judo debuted at the 1964 Tokyo Olympics and has been a mainstay since the 1972 Munich Games, with women's events starting at the 1992 Barcelona Paralympics. Japan has been particularly successful in Olympic judo, followed by France and South Korea. The Paris 2024 judo competitions will include various weight categories for both genders, culminating in a mixed team event. The Champ de Mars Arena, a temporary venue, will host these events during the Games. Judo remains a key aspect of the Olympic tradition, promoting excellence in both physical skill and moral values.

Modern pentathlon

The modern pentathlon, a contemporary version of the ancient pentathlon, was devised by Baron Pierre de Coubertin, the founder of the modern Olympic Games. It was inspired by the original pentathlon, which comprised running, jumping, javelin throw, discus throw, and wrestling. The modern iteration includes swimming, fencing, equestrian show jumping, and a combined running and shooting event known as the laser-run, overseen by the Union Internationale de Pentathlon Moderne (UIPM) established in 1948.

Participants compete in a 200m freestyle swim, engage in a fencing ranking round followed by a bonus round, and take part in show jumping on an unfamiliar horse. The laser-run, which combines running and shooting, serves as the final event, with athletes starting based on points accrued in the earlier disciplines. The first to finish the laser-run wins. The modern pentathlon has been part of the Olympic program since 1912 and transitioned to a one-day event, with the women's competition added in 2000. European nations, particularly Hungary and Sweden, have historically excelled in this sport. During the Paris 2024 Olympics, the modern pentathlon will be held over four days, with the Château de Versailles hosting the riding, fencing bonus round, swimming, and laser-run. The fencing ranking round will take place at the North Paris Arena (Villepinte), adding to the event's grandeur. The contemporary pentathlon stands as a testament to the Olympic agenda, demanding a blend of athletic strength, psychological resilience, and a range of competencies, thus positioning it among the most demanding and enthralling events in the sporting lineup.

Rowing

Rowing, which once served as a practical means of transport in early civilizations, evolved into a sport of competition in England during the latter part of the 17th century and the beginning of the 18th century. The inception of significant rowing contests was signified by the renowned Oxford-Cambridge boat race that commenced in 1828. In the sport of rowing, competitors drive boats by manipulating oars that are affixed to the craft, all while seated and facing away from their direction of travel. Standard races span a course of 2,000 meters, with participants either rowing solo or in crews of two, four, or eight. The two primary categories are double scull and sweep rowing. Sweep rowing involves each rower using both hands to operate a single oar, whereas sculling requires rowers to wield an oar in each hand. In the eight-person team configuration, a coxswain is responsible for directing and steering the boat via a rudder manipulated by their feet.

Since the inaugural modern Olympic Games in Athens in 1896, rowing has been featured, with the inclusion of women's competitions beginning in 1976. Initially, the United States dominated Olympic rowing, but later, countries such as the Soviet Union and Germany became prominent. Celebrated rowers like Sir Steve Redgrave and Elisabeta Oleniuc-Lipă have earned recognition as some of the most outstanding Olympic rowers, with numerous gold medals accredited to them. The rowing schedule for the upcoming Paris 2024 Olympics is set from July 27th to August 3rd and will include 14 events like single sculls, coxless pairs, and eights, among others. These events will be hosted at the Vaires-sur-Marne Nautical Stadium. Rowing maintains its allure with a combination of physical prowess, cooperative spirit, and storied tradition, solidifying its place within the Olympic Games.

Rugby

Originating from medieval European practices, rugby was formalized into modern codes between 1845 and 1848, thanks to the efforts of students at Rugby School in England and the University of Cambridge. The establishment of the first national federation in 1871 and the creation of the International Rugby Board (presently known as World Rugby) in 1886 provided a structured framework for the sport. Rugby is played in several variations, but the two principal forms are the 15-player rugby union and rugby sevens. Both adhere to basic rules concerning tackles, backward passing, and scrums, with adaptations according to the number of players engaged. Rugby sevens is distinguished by its swift pace and brief 14-minute matches, demanding high levels of fitness and agility from the athletes. Rugby's Olympic history has been intermittent, with rugby union appearing in the 1900, 1908, 1920, and 1924 Games. Since its reintroduction at the 2016 Rio Olympics in the sevens format, New Zealand and Fiji have claimed gold in the women's and men's categories, respectively, at the 2021 Games.

During the Paris 2024 Olympics, the rugby events will unfold from July 24th to July 30th, featuring both women's and men's rugby sevens. These events will be held at the Stade de France, setting the stage for exhilarating matches. Rugby continues to engage audiences globally with its storied past, widespread appeal, and dynamic play, ensuring its prominence in the Olympic Games.

Sailing

Sailing, tracing its competitive origins to the 19th century, made its international debut with the America's Cup in 1851, a race won by the schooner America from the New York Yacht Club. This triumph led to the trophy being renamed The America's Cup, marking the start of international sailing contests. Olympic sailing requires athletes to maneuver boats using only wind power, demonstrating their skill in ever-changing conditions. Overseen by World Sailing, the sport's international governing body, the typical format is fleet racing, where identical boats vie against each other on diverse courses. The Tokyo Games showcased ten sailing events, including windsurfing and the mixed Nacra 17 Foiling. The 2024 Olympic Games will introduce new categories like the windsurfer – iQFoil and kiteboarding, reflecting a shift toward more compact, agile vessels that demand greater athletic and technical prowess from sailors. Sailing has been a consistent feature of the Olympic Games since its inclusion in the 1900 Paris event, with the exception of the 1896 Athens Games, which were affected by weather conditions. Throughout the years, the sailing classes featured at the Olympics have evolved and are categorized by one-design specifications related to size and weight.

The 2024 Olympics will host sailing events from July 28th to August 8th in the scenic setting of the Marseille Marina, with competitions in women's, men's, and mixed classes.

Sailing's rich heritage, tactical complexity, and enduring popularity ensure its continued presence in the Olympic Games, captivating spectators around the globe.

Shooting

Shooting, with deep European roots and centuries-old traditions, has been a mainstay of the Olympic Games from their beginning. As a sport, shooting has gained international recognition, with competitors from over 100 countries participating in the Olympic shooting disciplines.

The sport includes three main disciplines: rifle, pistol, and shotgun. Rifle and pistol competitions are held on ranges with targets set at distances of 10m, 25m, and 50m. Competitors use relaxation techniques to stabilize their aim and accurately hit the bullseye. Shotgun events, conducted outdoors, challenge marksmen to hit aerial targets from various trajectories, demanding quick reflexes and strategic prowess. Shooting has featured in every Olympic Games, with the exceptions of 1904 and 1928. The number of shooting events has expanded over time, with 15 slated for the 2024 Olympics. The United States has historically led the medal tally, followed by China and Russia (under the USSR flag), with Italy also demonstrating strong performances in recent Games. The 2024 Olympic shooting events are scheduled from July 27th to August 5th at the National Shooting Center in Chateauroux, pending approval and agreements. The competitions will encompass events such as 10m Air Rifle, 50m Rifle 3 Positions, and Skeet, providing a stage for athletes to pursue Olympic distinction. Shooting's intricate history, technical demands, and global following ensure its continued significance in the Olympic Games, mesmerizing spectators with exhibitions of precision, concentration, and athletic skill.

Table tennis

Originally a pastime for the English elite, table tennis has transformed into an international sensation, with over 40 million enthusiasts, particularly in Asia and notably China. This sport has progressed from rudimentary beginnings to a high-tech competition with advanced rackets and lightweight balls.

Table tennis, a game marked by speed and excitement, is played across a net-divided table. Singles confrontations are generally a race to win four out of seven games, while team events consist of four singles and one doubles match. Victory in a game is achieved by the first to 11 points, with a two-point lead necessary. Making its Olympic entrance in Seoul in 1988, table tennis began with men's and women's singles and doubles. The

Olympic roster has since grown to include mixed doubles and team events, promoting equal participation. Chinese competitors have largely dominated, securing the bulk of Olympic golds. The 2024 Olympic table tennis competitions will take place from July 27 to August 10 at the South Paris Arena, with men's and women's singles, teams, and mixed doubles events. The International Table Tennis Federation (ITTF) governs this sport, fostering its global progression.

Table tennis remains a captivating sport with a storied past, enthralling global audiences and highlighting the prowess and precision of its players at the Olympic level.

Taekwondo

Taekwondo, Korea's legacy of "the way of kicking and punching," has evolved from ancient martial arts like taekkyon. It rose to prominence in Korea in the early 20th century and went international with the establishment of World Taekwondo (WT) in 1973 and the first World Championships in Seoul that year. In taekwondo, competitors score by landing precise kicks and punches while evading their opponent's strikes. Contests are held on an octagonal mat and consist of three two-minute rounds. Points reflect the complexity of the techniques, with head kicks and spinning kicks scoring higher. Penalties can be imposed for infractions.

Debuting as a demonstration sport at Seoul in 1988, taekwondo became a full Olympic event in Sydney 2000. While initially Korean-dominated, the sport now sees champions from a diverse array of nations. The 2024 Olympic taekwondo events will occur from August 7 to August 10 at Paris's Grand Palais, where athletes will vie for medals across various weight classes. World Taekwondo ensures the sport's international growth and appeal.

Tennis

Tennis, tracing its origins to the medieval French "jeu de paume," became popular in 19th-century England, leading to the creation of the International Lawn Tennis Federation (ILTF) in 1913. Olympic tennis features men's and women's singles and doubles, with singles often decided in the best of three sets, employing tie-breaks for deadlocked sets.

After an inconsistent Olympic presence and exclusion post-1924 due to professionalism disputes, tennis made a permanent comeback in Seoul 1988. Since then, tennis greats like Rafael Nadal, Stan Wawrinka, Roger Federer, and the Williams sisters have graced the Olympic courts. The 2024 Olympic tennis competitions will be hosted from July 27 to

August 4 at Roland-Garros Stadium in Paris, where athletes will strive for Olympic success on this renowned tennis stage.

Triathlon

Triathlon, blending swimming, cycling, and running, originated in the 1970s as a novel workout by the San Diego Track Club, with the first official event in 1974. Its popularity led to the International Triathlon Union's (ITU) formation in 1989 and the inaugural Triathlon World Championships. The Olympic triathlon consists of a 1500 m swim, a 40 km bike ride, and a 10 km run for both men and women, with the winner being the first to finish. Introduced in Tokyo 2020, the mixed relay adds a new layer of excitement, with teams of two men and two women each tackling a short-course triathlon. Since its Olympic debut in Sydney 2000, triathlon has awarded 39 medals across six Games to athletes from 16 countries, showcasing the sport's widespread appeal. The 2024 Olympic triathlon will take place on July 30, July 31, and August 5 at the Pont Alexandre III in Paris, offering a scenic backdrop for this grueling competition.

Volleyball

Volleyball, an energetic team sport, emerged in 1895 at Springfield College, Massachusetts, thanks to the creative efforts of William G. Morgan. Initially termed "mintonette," the game was intended as a less strenuous sport suitable for older participants. Its appeal quickly expanded, reaching nations such as Canada, Cuba, and Japan by the early 20th century. The formation of the International Volleyball Federation (FIVB) in 1947 marked a significant milestone, followed by the first World Championships for men in 1949 and for women in 1952.

The sport consists of two teams with six players each, facing off on an 18-meter by 9-meter indoor court. Matches are generally contested in a best-of-five set format, with sets going to 25 points. In the event of a 2-2 set tie, a decisive fifth set is played to 15 points. Volleyball is characterized by high-speed exchanges that can see the ball soar at speeds up to 130 km/h, demanding rapid reflexes and formidable defensive abilities from the athletes. Volleyball's Olympic journey began at the 1964 Tokyo Games. The initial championship-style competition, where all teams competed against one another, later evolved into a conventional tournament format with pool play leading to knockout rounds. Over the years, countries such as the Soviet Union, Cuba, Italy, China, and Brazil have shown remarkable prowess in volleyball, with the former Soviet Union, Brazil, and the United States topping the medal count with over ten medals each.

The volleyball competitions at the upcoming 2024 Olympic Games in Paris are scheduled from July 27th to August 11th at the South Paris Arena, featuring both women's and men's events. The FIVB remains the sport's global governing authority.

Beach volleyball

Beach volleyball, an exciting variant of the game played on sand, originated in Santa Monica, California. The first beach volleyball tournament in 1947 and the establishment of an initial circuit in the 1950s attracted numerous players to California's shores. The 1980s saw the professionalization of the sport, culminating in the FIVB's sanctioning of its first international tournament in 1987.

Beach volleyball is played by two teams of two on a 16-meter by 8-meter sand court. The game is divided into sets, with a match victory awarded to the first team to win two sets, played to 21 points each, with a tiebreaker set to 15 points if necessary. The sport demands exceptional agility and adaptability from the athletes, as they must cover more terrain with only two players per side. Outdoor conditions such as wind and sunlight add another layer of challenge to the game. Beach volleyball officially entered the Olympic program at the 1996 Atlanta Games, following its exhibition in Barcelona in 1992. Brazil and the USA have been particularly successful, claiming a combined 24 Olympic medals, including 10 golds. The Paris 2024 Olympics will host beach volleyball events between July 27th and August 10th at a temporary Eiffel Tower Stadium, set against a picturesque Parisian backdrop.

Diving

Diving, with roots in 19th-century Sweden and Germany, evolved from gymnastic displays into water, emphasizing acrobatics and elegance. Swedish divers introduced their art to Great Britain, leading to the foundation of the Amateur Diving Association in 1901. Olympic diving features both the 3-meter springboard and the 10-meter platform events, with individual and synchronized contests judged on aesthetics, complexity, and water entry. The USA initially led the field, but China has since become a dominant force. The Paris 2024 Olympics will host diving from July 27th to August 10th at the Aquatics Centre, the sole permanent sports venue constructed for the occasion, also accommodating artistic swimming and water polo.

Marathon swimming

Marathon swimming has its origins in the early modern Olympic Games, where swimming events were held in natural waters until 1908. The sport's official inclusion in the FINA World Swimming Championships came in 1991 with a 25km race. The 10km event debuted at the 2001 Championships in Fukuoka, Japan. Marathon swimming, now an Olympic event since the 2008 Beijing Games, tests athletes' endurance and strategic acumen in open water settings. The marathon swimming competitions for the 2024 Paris Olympics are set for August 8th and 9th at the Pont Alexandre III, offering a historic panorama for the endurance event.

Artistic swimming

Artistic swimming, a fusion of aquatic acrobatics and music, originally included male competitors but has since become predominantly female-oriented. Its rise to fame in the United States during the early 1900s led to the establishment of formal competitions. In the Olympics, artistic swimming features two categories: duet and team. Competitors perform both a free and a technical routine in each category, judged on execution, synchronization, level of difficulty, musical interpretation, and choreography. The sport is conducted in a pool with dimensions of 3 meters in depth, 25 meters in length, and 20 meters in width, where swimmers showcase their remarkable flexibility, strength, precision, and coordination. Making its Olympic debut at the 1984 Los Angeles Games, artistic swimming will see male athletes participate in the team event for the first time at the Paris 2024 Games. The United States and Canada initially led the discipline, securing 17 medals, including eight golds. However, since the 2000 Sydney Games, the Russian Olympic Committee has become the predominant force, securing 12 consecutive gold medals. The Paris 2024 artistic swimming events are slated for August 5-10 at the Aquatics Centre, the only permanent facility constructed for these Games. The center will also host water polo and diving.

Swimming

Swimming, tracing its origins to prehistoric times, became a competitive pursuit in the 19th century with the founding of the National Swimming Society in Great Britain. Although breaststroke was the initial stroke of choice, other styles have since been introduced and are now mainstays of Olympic competition.

Olympic swimming contests are held in a 50-meter pool, featuring four strokes: breaststroke, butterfly, backstroke, and freestyle, with the crawl being the most common freestyle technique. The mixed medley relay incorporates all four strokes, challenging athletes to seamlessly transition between them across various distances, from 50-meter sprints to 1500-meter long-distance races. Competitors must exhibit explosive speed, endurance, strength, and technical skill. Since the inception of the modern Olympic Games, swimming has been a fundamental event. Although the earliest races took place in open water, pool-based events have been standard since the 1908 London Games, which prompted the creation of the International Swimming Federation (FINA). The United States has historically been the dominant nation in Olympic swimming, amassing over 250 gold medals.

From July 27 to August 4, the Paris La Défense Arena in Nanterre will play host to the Paris 2024 swimming events. Known for its concerts and rugby matches, this venue will be transformed into an Olympic pool for the first time, accommodating a significant audience for a series of freestyle, backstroke, breaststroke, butterfly, and individual medley races, as well as relays for both genders.

Water polo

Water polo, which began as a water-based form of rugby in England during the mid-19th century, was standardized in 1870 by the London Swimming Association, leading to a style of play more akin to football. The sport's first international match was held in 1890 between England and Scotland.

Today's water polo involves two teams of seven players each, competing in a pool that adheres to FINA's recommended dimensions. Games are divided into four eight-minute quarters, with teams having 30 seconds of possession time. The sport permits physical contact, requiring players to possess strength, stamina, tactical acumen, and physical prowess. Water polo boasts a long Olympic tradition, having been introduced at the 1900 Games alongside rugby, with the women's event added at the Sydney 2000 Games. European nations, particularly Hungary, have excelled in the men's category, while the United States has dominated the women's event in recent Olympics. The Paris La Défense Arena in Nanterre will transform into a water polo arena from August 5-11 for the Paris 2024 Games, inviting audiences to experience the exhilarating matches.

Weightlifting

Weightlifting, with historical roots in ancient Egypt and Greece, was revived as an organized sport in the 19th century and gained international recognition. Olympic weightlifting challenges athletes to perform two lifts: the snatch and the clean and jerk. The snatch requires lifting the barbell overhead in a single motion, and the clean and jerk involves raising the barbell to the shoulders before thrusting it overhead. These techniques test the competitors' physical power and mental fortitude. Participants are given three attempts at each lift, with their best performances combined for a total score. For Paris 2024, weightlifters will compete in five weight categories for both men and women.

Since its inclusion in the inaugural modern Olympic Games in Athens 1896, weightlifting has featured consistently, with women's events introduced at the Sydney 2000 Games. The sport has seen various countries, including European nations, the Soviet Union, and China, achieve dominance over the years. The South Paris Arena will host the weightlifting competitions from August 7-11 during the Paris 2024 Olympics, under the governance of the International Weightlifting Federation.

Wrestling

Wrestling stands as one of the most ancient athletic disciplines, with its origins traceable to early civilizations such as the Sumerians. It was a prominent feature of the ancient Olympic Games, first appearing in 708 BC, and continues to be a vital element of the Olympic tradition. In contemporary wrestling, there are two main forms: Greco-Roman wrestling, which is deeply connected to historical practices, and freestyle wrestling, which is a relatively modern variant. In the domain of Greco-Roman wrestling, participants are restricted to using their arms and upper bodies when engaging in offense. Conversely, freestyle wrestling permits the utilization of legs and the ability to grip adversaries both above and below the waistline. The objective in both variants is to immobilize the adversary's shoulders against the mat or accumulate points by executing takedowns and reversals, all within two rounds lasting three minutes each.

Since the modern Olympic Games' revival in 1896, wrestling has been a fixture, with Greco-Roman wrestling debuting then and freestyle wrestling introduced in 1904. The Olympic roster expanded to include women's freestyle wrestling in 2004. Historically, athletes from the Soviet Union have dominated the wrestling scene, securing a multitude of medals, with the United States not far behind. In the realm of women's wrestling,

Japan has consistently been at the forefront of Olympic success. The wrestling schedule for the Paris 2024 Olympics includes events in women's freestyle, men's Greco-Roman, and men's freestyle, spanning various weight divisions. These contests are set to unfold at the Champ de Mars Arena, spanning from the 5th to the 11th of August.

Star athletes to watch and their stories

As the world eagerly anticipates the 2024 Paris Olympic Games, the sporting community is abuzz with excitement at the prospect of witnessing a new wave of athletic prodigies. The Games are set to be a stage for showcasing exceptional talent and intense rivalry across a multitude of disciplines, from the track and swimming pool to the gymnastics mat and basketball court. Within this cohort of exceptional athletes, certain individuals have already distinguished themselves on the international scene. These prodigies from various nations epitomize the zenith of sports mastery and are the embodiment of the enduring Olympic values of resilience, excellence, and fair play. As the journey to Paris unfolds, it is fitting to turn the spotlight on these extraordinary sportspeople and honor their remarkable abilities as they endeavor to secure their legacy in the annals of Olympic history.

Among the notable U.S. athletes expected to leave a mark at the Paris 2024 Olympics is Sha'Carri Richardson. Her stellar track and field performances in 2023 have captured widespread attention. Having rebounded from a suspension that prevented her participation in the Tokyo 2020 Olympics, Richardson has demonstrated her prowess by claiming victories in prominent sprint competitions over the years. Her crowning achievement was winning the 100m event at the World Championships in Budapest, where she set a new championship record. Eager to make her Olympic debut, Richardson is anticipated to be a strong competitor in Paris.

In the realm of swimming, Hunter Armstrong, also referred to as "The Magician," has made a splash with his extraordinary feats in 2023. Armstrong impressed the swimming community by securing a bronze medal in the 100m backstroke and a gold medal in the non-Olympic 50m backstroke at the World Aquatics Championships. His stellar performances have established him as an emerging talent in the swimming sphere, and he is poised to extend his success to the Olympic platform in Paris.

Switching to basketball, Jimmer Fredette has carved out a niche for himself in the 3x3 format. Despite his extensive experience in conventional basketball leagues, Fredette has adapted to the 3x3 game and led the U.S. team to victory at the Pan American Games. With his seasoned expertise and leadership, Fredette is focused on aiding Team USA in securing its inaugural men's 3x3 basketball medal at the Paris Olympics.

In gymnastics, Shilese Jones has risen as a formidable and accomplished competitor. Despite encountering challenges, including missing the 2020 Olympics and personal adversities, Jones has persisted and established herself as a premier gymnast. She contributed to the U.S. team's triumph at the world championships and earned individual medals in the all-around and bars categories. As the Olympic year approaches, Jones is driven to demonstrate her abilities and affirm her elite status in the sport.

Lastly, in wrestling, Zain Retherford has achieved significant milestones, highlighted by a gold medal win at the world championships in 2023. Following a silver medal performance the year prior, Retherford's triumph in 2023 signals him as a prime candidate for Olympic gold. With the U.S. Olympic Trials forthcoming, Retherford is motivated by the prospect of representing his nation and realizing his Olympic dreams.

Powerhouse Potential of the 2024 USA Basketball Team

The revelation of the 41-strong selection for the 2024 USA Basketball Men's National Team has generated a buzz of excitement and anticipation among enthusiasts, mentors, and athletes. Under the guidance of managing director Grant Hill and head coach Steve Kerr, the lineup boasts a formidable array of NBA luminaries, all geared up to leave a lasting impression at the Olympic Games in Paris. A standout feature of this selection is the blend of seasoned NBA professionals with emerging talents and youthful prospects. With elite players such as LeBron James, Kevin Durant, Stephen Curry, and Damian Lillard on the list, the USA team presents an unmatched combination of skill and experience. These experienced players contribute not only their remarkable on-court abilities but also their leadership qualities, proven track records, and a wealth of international experience from prior Olympic and FIBA events.

Joining these veterans are the likes of Jayson Tatum, Devin Booker, and Donovan Mitchell, the new generation of stars already leaving their mark in the NBA and ready to become the new faces of Team USA. Their presence in the selection highlights the depth of American basketball talent and reflects the strategic approach of combining youthful energy with veteran savvy to excel internationally. The pool's diversity and adaptability provide Coach Kerr and his team with a plethora of strategic choices and the ability to craft lineups that can exploit the weaknesses of adversaries while enhancing Team USA's own strengths. The players' ability to fill various roles and adapt to different playing styles allows the team to dynamically adjust their strategy to counteract rivals' tactics. Team chemistry and unity, fostered during training camps and exhibition matches, will be pivotal for Team USA's prospects in Paris. Building a unified squad with a shared vision and a commitment to uphold national pride is vital for triumphing over the globe's premier basketball contingents.

Additionally, the chance to perform on an international platform and vie for Olympic gold is a compelling incentive for these athletes. For numerous NBA stars, securing an Olympic gold is a career zenith and an opportunity to secure their legacy alongside the pantheon of basketball greats who have represented the USA. The assemblage of star NBA athletes in the 2024 USA Basketball Men's National Team selection holds the promise of a significant impact at the Paris

Olympics. With their extraordinary abilities, rich experience, and unwavering commitment to national representation, they capture the essence of Team USA and are fully equipped to chase Olympic triumph on the global stage.

Attending the Games in Paris

Ticketing Information: Securing Your Seat at the Paris 2024 Games

Experiencing the Olympics firsthand is an unparalleled opportunity, and the Paris 2024 Games are set to continue this tradition. For those eager to be part of this momentous occasion, here is a structured approach to obtaining tickets:

Primary Source for Tickets:

Visit the Paris 2024 Official Ticketing Site: The only reliable avenue for authentic tickets is the official Paris 2024 website at https://www.paris2024.org/en/tickets/. Exercise caution with third-party vendors to avoid counterfeit or inflated tickets.

Stages of Ticket Sales:

- Initial Lottery Phase (Concluded as of December 2023): The first stage involved a registration for a lottery, with chosen participants given a specific timeframe to purchase tickets.
- Secondary Market Phase (Launching in Spring 2024): The Games will introduce an official platform for the resale of tickets. Stay vigilant for announcements regarding the launch date by monitoring the official site.
- Final Sales Phase (During the Games): Tickets not yet sold will be available on a rolling basis, sold as they become available.

Variety of Ticket Options:

- Event-Specific Tickets: Select tickets for particular events that align with your preferences and financial plan.
- Bundled Packages: Opt for curated packages that provide access to a series of events or cater to particular sporting categories.
- Exclusive Hospitality Packages: These packages offer top-tier tickets coupled with perks such as gourmet dining, access to private lounges, and expedited entry.

Key Points to Remember:

Registration on the Official Site: Set up an account on the official ticketing platform in advance of the sales phases.

Identification Requirements: Have your identification ready for the ticket purchasing process.

Payment Options: Review the payment methods accepted to ensure a seamless purchase experience.

Ticket Purchase Limits: Note the restrictions on the quantity of tickets you can buy per person or event.

Staying Informed:

Consistently consult the Paris 2024 official website and follow their social media for the latest news on ticket availability and sales phases. Sign up for the official newsletter to receive prompt updates and essential announcements. Adhering to this guidance and staying abreast of the latest information will help you successfully acquire tickets to the Paris 2024 Olympic Games, where you can witness the excitement of athletic excellence in person.

Venues: Locations, access, and amenities

As the international community keenly anticipates the grandeur of the Paris 2024 Olympic Games, the buzz is not solely about the showcase of athletic talent but also about the storied settings that will host these monumental competitions. Paris, a city steeped in history with its stunning vistas, is set to transform its avenues, green spaces, and celebrated sites into stages for Olympic glory.

Iconic monuments like the Eiffel Tower and the historic Palace of Versailles will provide a dramatic canvas for the athletes' endeavors. Imagine beach volleyball being played in the shadow of the Eiffel Tower or horse riders competing amidst Versailles' opulence—each location offers a distinct and memorable stage for participants and onlookers.

Beyond the city's borders, France and its territories are poised to welcome the globe's finest competitors. The renowned Stade de France will host track and field events, while Roland Garros, synonymous with the French Open, will accommodate tennis and boxing, each venue contributing its rich sports history to the Games.

The idyllic setting of French Polynesia, too, calls to surfers to etch their mark in its blue waves. With the Olympic spirit spreading throughout France and its territories, a sense of unity and competitive fervor will be felt universally, uniting spectators and athletes worldwide.

The forthcoming 2024 Olympics is set to be a grand celebration, encapsulating France's cultural depth and varied topography. The events will span across Paris, the Île-de-France, and other regions, inviting visitors to explore the expanse of France's beauty, from its ancient urban centers to its scenic rural expanses.

Paris, the heart of the Games and a global cultural hub, will host key events, including the opening and closing ceremonies. As a city renowned for its cultural offerings, Paris provides visitors with a rich tapestry of museums, art galleries, and culinary delights, all set against a backdrop of iconic landmarks.

The surrounding Île-de-France region will also be crucial to the Games, with venues like the Stade de France for athletics. This region is home to historic cities, quaint villages, and stunning landscapes, like the Château of Versailles and the Fontainebleau Forest, each offering a window into France's illustrious past and architectural splendor.

The Olympic events will reach beyond the Parisian region, allowing visitors to experience France's multifaceted regions and traditions. The French Alps and the Pyrenees will serve as magnificent settings for cycling events, while the Mediterranean coast will host sailing competitions, with Marseille as the scenic port city. Indoor sports like basketball will take place in venues such as the Bercy Arena.

The Paris 2024 Olympics presents a unique chance for visitors to traverse the diverse terrains and cultures of this captivating country. Whether one is a sports aficionado, a cultural connoisseur, or in pursuit of an unforgettable adventure, the French Olympics promise an array of experiences. Thus, all are invited to delve into France's multifaceted allure and partake in the thrill of the Games in one of the world's most picturesque nations.

Paris Regions

Grand Palais

The Grand Palais, a Parisian landmark, may not be the primary venue for the 2024 Olympics, but it will play a pivotal role in hosting a variety of Olympic and Paralympic events.

Undergoing refurbishments, this historical edifice will be the backdrop for sports such as fencing, taekwondo, wheelchair fencing, and para taekwondo. Meanwhile, the Grand Palais Éphémère, a provisional structure on the Champ de Mars mirroring the original's grandeur, will become the stage for these sports. Audiences will be captivated by the swift movements of fencers and the strength of taekwondo competitors, while the Paralympic athletes will demonstrate their extraordinary tenacity and skill. Although the Grand Palais will be partially accessible due to renovations, its nave and galleries will welcome visitors during the Games, merging the thrill of sport with the allure of cultural magnificence. Thus, the Grand Palais and its temporary counterpart will be central to the Games, offering spectators a fusion of athletic and cultural experiences.

Alexandre III Bridge

The Alexandre III Bridge will be transformed into a central hub for endurance sports during the Paris 2024 Olympic Games. Athletes will compete against the backdrop of this ornate bridge, beginning with marathon swimmers taking on the Seine River's currents. The triathlon will follow, with the bridge acting as a transition zone for the cycling segment. The bridge and its environs will also host the road cycling event, where cyclists will navigate a demanding course. The para triathlon will bring Paralympic athletes to the forefront, as they take on the same rigorous triathlon challenge. The Alexandre III Bridge will thus offer a stunning setting for these Olympic and Paralympic events, blending Parisian elegance with the spectacle of human endurance.

Porte de la Chapelle Arena

The Porte de la Chapelle Arena, a state-of-the-art facility in Paris, will host a variety of events during the 2024 Olympic and Paralympic Games. The arena will initially be the venue for badminton, a sport that requires swift reflexes and strategic play. It will then transition to rhythmic gymnastics, where gymnasts will dazzle with their grace and skill. After the Olympics, the arena will accommodate para-badminton and para-powerlifting, highlighting the perseverance and excellence of Paralympic athletes. Designed with accessibility in mind, the arena will celebrate the diversity of human performance and the spirit of inclusivity. As such, the Porte de la Chapelle Arena will be more than a sports venue; it will be a beacon of athletic prowess and human aspiration, showcasing the elegance and intensity of competitive sports in various forms.

Parc Urbain La Concorde

In 2024, the heart of Paris will be transformed into a lively hub for urban sports at the Parc Urbain La Concorde. This temporary facility, with a 10,000-spectator capacity, will buzz with the excitement of BMX freestyle, skateboarding, breakdancing, and 3x3 basketball competitions.

Set against the historic backdrop of Place de la Concorde, with the Champs-Élysées and the Tuileries Gardens nearby, the park will merge city vibes with grandeur. Picture athletes performing stunning aerial stunts and defying gravity with the Paris skyline in view.

BMX freestyle competitors will demonstrate their agility and flair on a specially constructed course, complete with ramps and obstacles. Skateboarders will then turn the plaza into a showcase of creativity and technical skill, their boards echoing against the pavement as they execute their tricks.

Breakdancing, a fresh addition to the Olympic roster, will bring its dynamic beat to the venue, while 3x3 basketball will offer a swift, strategic version of the classic game. The Parc Urbain La Concorde will be more than just a sports venue; it will be a cultural melting pot, bringing together fans, athletes, and artists for a memorable Olympic experience.

The Trocadéro

The Trocadéro will serve as a stunning setting for road cycling and athletics during the 2024 Games, providing a view of the Eiffel Tower and the Seine. Elite athletes will compete on a course weaving through Paris, with the Trocadéro gardens later converted into a temporary stadium for track and field events. This venue will not only host breathtaking athletic feats but also offer a peaceful retreat and cultural enrichment at nearby museums.

The Eiffel Tower Stadium

The Eiffel Tower Stadium, set in the Champ de Mars, will host beach volleyball and blind football in a temporary arena with over 12,000 seats. The stadium will be a beacon of excitement and inclusion, showcasing the talents of athletes in both the Olympics and Paralympics. It will also emphasize sustainability and offer visitors a chance to enjoy the Games in the shadow of one of Paris's most iconic landmarks.

During the 2024 Paris Olympic Games, the Hôtel des Invalides, commonly known as Les Invalides, extends its significance beyond being a mere historical site. Initially established as a residence for injured soldiers, this distinguished structure is repurposed into a dynamic venue for multiple sports, encompassing archery, track and field, road cycling, and para archery events.

Les Invalides

Les Invalides serves not only as an Olympic venue but also as a gateway to French cultural heritage. Within its walls, visitors can explore the Musée de l'Armée, which chronicles France's military past, and the Dôme des Invalides, the final resting place of Napoleon Bonaparte. This melding of cultural depth with the Olympic spirit offers guests a chance to immerse themselves in France's legacy while engaging with the excitement of the Games. In essence, Les Invalides extends beyond its function as a sports venue; it stands as a testament to perseverance, the breadth of human achievement, and cultural wealth. The convergence of varied sports disciplines and the historic essence of the site promise an unparalleled experience at the 2024 Paris Olympic Games.

The Cour d'Honneur

The Cour d'Honneur, Les Invalides' primary courtyard, is set to be the enthralling backdrop for the archery events. It will accommodate an audience of 5,000, offering them the chance to observe the concentration and skill of the archers as they compete for Olympic medals against a setting steeped in history. The athletes' meticulous skill and intense focus are anticipated to offer an absorbing spectacle. Additionally, the Cour d'Honneur will be repurposed to welcome the para archery competition, accommodating an audience of 5,000. The exceptional prowess and resolve of the para-archers in their quest for Paralympic success will bring an extra dimension of awe to this venue of historical significance.

The Champ de Mars

Adjacent to the historic Les Invalides and situated on the Champ de Mars, a bespoke stadium with a 20,000-seat capacity is slated for construction to accommodate the athletics events. This modern arena will be the backdrop for a spectrum of track and field competitions, ranging from the electrifying 100-meter dash to the endurance-testing marathon. Here, athletes will be pushing the boundaries of their abilities in pursuit of triumph, inspired by the nearby historical monuments. The surrounding boulevards and avenues of Les Invalides will not just serve as scenery but as the challenging route for the road cycling event. As cyclists navigate the intricate circuit, they will display a combination of tactical skill and shear strength. The course will meander through Paris's core, offering spectators fleeting views of famed sites, and will reach its finale in the vicinity of Les Invalides.

Roland-Garros

The esteemed Stade Roland-Garros, with a seating capacity of 15,000, is gearing up to serve as the focal point of athletic prowess for the 2024 Olympic Games. This venerable stadium, with its deep-rooted connections to the world of tennis, is celebrated for its distinctive red clay courts and the fervent support of its Parisian spectators. It is set to host the Olympic tennis tournament where the world's premier athletes will converge to compete on this time-honored surface, each striving to secure a place in the annals of Olympic history. In addition to its storied tennis tradition, Roland-Garros is embracing a spirit of progress and inclusiveness. The arena will also accommodate the Olympic boxing events, transforming its space to include a provisional boxing ring. This will provide a platform for amateur pugilists to display their prowess, strength, and competitive zeal as they contend for the coveted Olympic gold amidst a charged environment. Moreover, the spotlight will shine on wheelchair tennis at Roland-Garros, underscoring the commitment and skill of Paralympic competitors. The courts will be specially modified to meet the needs of wheelchair-bound athletes, ensuring equitable and rigorous competition. Observing their unyielding spirit and outstanding abilities as they vie for Paralympic honors is set to be an awe-inspiring spectacle.

Roland-Garros extends an experience that surpasses the exhilaration of sports. The site is home to a museum that celebrates tennis's storied past, offering guests a chance to immerse themselves in the heritage of the game. The adjacent Jardin des Serres d'Auteuil also provides a serene haven, offering a moment of relaxation and an appreciation for the picturesque Parisian landscape. Thus, Roland-Garros transcends its function as merely an Olympic venue; it stands as a beacon of heritage, modernity, and inclusivity. The opportunity to witness a variety of sports and engage with the rich historical and cultural features of the setting ensures a memorable journey during the Paris 2024 Olympic Games.

The Parc des Princes

The renowned Parc des Princes, traditionally the bastion of the esteemed Paris Saint-Germain football team, is set to serve as a dynamic platform for the football events of the 2024 Olympic Games. This celebrated arena, famed for its fervent local supporters and charged ambiance, is poised to host a display of sporting excellence and patriotic fervor on its revered grounds. Envision the exuberant cheers as elite football players take to the field at the Parc des Princes. Prepare to be captivated by the thrilling exhibition of finesse, strength, and strategic acumen as nations vie for dominance on this legendary pitch. The interaction of every movement, linkage of play, and goal attempt will be infused with an intense vitality, forging a memorable spectacle for both athletes and fans.

The Parc des Princes extends beyond the spectacle of sport, offering a gateway to the cultural heartbeat of Paris. Situated in the lively 16th district, the stadium invites visitors to delve into the local ambiance, indulge in the finest French gastronomy, and absorb the city's dynamic spirit. For aficionados of the beautiful game, the Parc des Princes is a hallowed destination. The opportunity to observe some of the globe's premier talent on a field graced by footballing titans such as Zlatan Ibrahimović and Kylian Mbappé is an experience that promises to be etched in memory. The venue transcends mere sport, epitomizing the spirit of Parisian ardor and soccer distinction. Thus, experiencing an Olympic football event at the Parc des Princes is an unparalleled encounter. The combination of a charged atmosphere, the exquisite display of football on the field, and the enveloping Parisian backdrop ensures a chapter of the Olympic narrative that will be treasured forever.

South Paris Arena

The South Paris Arena, with a seating capacity of 15,000, will morph into a dynamic center for various sports during the 2024 Olympic and Paralympic Games. Spectators will have the opportunity to observe competitors demonstrate their power, accuracy, and tactical acumen in a series of events, ranging from the intense displays of weightlifting to the swift exchanges in volleyball. Initially, the venue will be reconfigured to accommodate the weightlifting events, where top-tier athletes will challenge their physical boundaries by lifting the heaviest weights they can in both the snatch and clean and jerk categories. As competitors strive for new personal records and possibly Olympic milestones, the crowd's applause will fill the air, reflecting their awe of the athletes' immense power and concentration. Subsequently, the venue will shift its setup for the handball matches. This high-speed, energetic team sport will highlight the athletes' remarkable physical prowess, collaborative effort, and strategic gameplay as they vie for victory on the court. The charged ambiance, combined with the players' nimbleness and tactical ingenuity, is set to keep the audience riveted. As the games progress, the arena will be readied for volleyball matches. Audiences can expect to see precise teamwork and forceful spikes as teams engage in this exhilarating game. The court, bisected by a net, becomes the backdrop for strategic exchanges, agile saves, and suspenseful plays, with the venue's design ensuring spectators don't miss a moment of the action. The arena will also serve as the venue for table tennis, where attendees can marvel at the competitors' rapid reflexes, precision, and strategic prowess as they partake in swift rallies. The rhythmic sound of the ball against the paddles and the athletes' quick tactical decisions will offer an engrossing spectacle.

Additionally, the South Paris Arena will host boccia, a Paralympic sport that emphasizes precision and is akin to bocce ball, tailored for athletes with impairments. Observing the tenacity and finesse of para-athletes as they contend for Paralympic honors is set to be an uplifting experience. The venue will further adapt to accommodate para table tennis, welcoming para-athletes as they display their exceptional abilities, utilizing modified equipment and demonstrating their resilient spirit in high-level competition. The collective cheers of the audience will echo throughout, celebrating the athletes' commitment and skill. In its final adaptation, the arena will present goalball, a Paralympic sport designed for visually impaired athletes. This sport, which relies on sound and necessitates extraordinary teamwork, communication, and spatial orientation, will offer an inspiring view of the athletes' resolve and strategic gameplay.

Thus, the South Paris Arena transcends its function as merely a sports facility; it becomes an emblem of diversity, athletic prowess, and the breadth of human capability. The array of sports and the indomitable spirit of both able-bodied competitors and para-athletes are set to deliver an unparalleled experience at the Paris 2024 Games.

Hôtel de Ville

The esteemed Hôtel de Ville in Paris is set to become an extraordinary arena for the track and field events of the 2024 Olympic Games. This venue, rich with French heritage and architectural splendor, is poised to host a spectacle of athleticism, showcasing the pinnacle of human performance in a city renowned for its allure. Envision the vibrant atmosphere as the world's top athletes engage in track and field competitions. With its classic Renaissance design, the Hôtel de Ville will be both the commencement and culmination site for various races, providing a memorable and scenic environment. Anticipate the thrill of the sprint finals on a specially constructed track for the occasion, or support marathon participants as they course through Paris's historic avenues, with landmarks like the Louvre and Notre Dame Cathedral enhancing the route.

Incorporating the Hôtel de Ville into the Olympic festivities is a testament to the blend of athletic excellence with the cultural and historical fabric of Paris. It allows spectators to immerse themselves in the Olympic ethos within the city's storied core, nurturing a profound bond between the Games and the inhabitants of Paris. Additionally, the adjacent streets will be converted into dynamic hubs for fans, replete with a variety of amusements and activities. Attendees will have the opportunity to engage with the Olympic atmosphere through hands-on exhibits, artistic showcases, and the chance to mingle with a global community of sports aficionados. Thus, the Hôtel de Ville elevates beyond merely being a sports venue; it epitomizes the exchange of cultures, the zeal for sports, and the resilient essence of Paris. The convergence of athletic excellence and Parisian historical context is set to deliver an unparalleled and memorable chapter in the 2024 Olympic Games.

Bercy Arena

The Bercy Arena, noted for its dynamic ambiance, will morph into a hub of athletic excellence for the 2024 Olympic and Paralympic Games. Anticipate a range of sportsmanship, from the aerial elegance of gymnastics to the cooperative precision of basketball, all amplified by the venue's vibrant pulse.

Initially, the Bercy Arena will be reconfigured to accommodate the basketball tournaments. Prepare to be enthralled by the rapid pace, remarkable agility, and tactical acumen of elite basketball contenders as they vie on the hardwood. The roar of the crowd will fill the air as teams vie for Olympic glory. Subsequent to the basketball events, the venue will be reimagined for the artistic gymnastics contests. The setting will be primed for gymnasts to display their extraordinary suppleness, power, and poise through complex sequences on the uneven bars, balance beam, and vault. The spectacle of their soaring stunts and expressive performances is set to be a mesmerizing highlight.

Following this, the Bercy Arena will open its doors to the trampoline gymnastics athletes. This energetic discipline requires superb poise, strength, and spatial acumen as competitors execute flips, twists, and somersaults on a trampoline. The audience's applause will echo as gymnasts challenge the limits of physical dexterity. Post the Olympic festivities, the Bercy Arena will serve as a stage for para-athletes to demonstrate their incredible abilities and resolute spirit. The wheelchair basketball matches will feature athletes displaying impressive cooperation, strategic execution, and skill on a modified court. The venue will transform into an arena of inspiration and triumph as para-athletes contend for Paralympic honors.

Thus, the Bercy Arena will elevate beyond a mere sports facility. It will stand as a beacon of human capability, sporting variety, and indomitable resolve. The enthralling athletic performances across both Olympic and Paralympic disciplines are set to offer an indelible experience at the Paris 2024 Games.

Île-de-France regions

Yves-du-Manoir Stadium

The venerable Stade Yves-du-Manoir, with a seating capacity of 18,000 and set against the idyllic backdrop of Bois de Vincennes in Paris, is set to come alive as the epicenter of field hockey for the 2024 Olympic Games. Anticipate a captivating showcase of agility, tactical prowess, and superior skill on the synthetic pitch as national teams vie for the ultimate title in this exhilarating sport.

Envision the arena resonating with the roar of the crowd as athletes demonstrate masterful control of the stick, propel the ball at breakneck speeds, and craft ingenious plays to outmaneuver their rivals. The charged ambience, amplified by the stakes of the games, ensures a gripping spectator experience with every match.

Moreover, Stade Yves-du-Manoir stands as a monument to France's sporting heritage. Constructed in 1906, it has been the stage for numerous athletic feats, including the rugby events of the 1924 Olympics. The current hockey contests offer attendees a chance to engage with the storied past of French athletic endeavors and the timeless ethos of the Olympics.

Adjacent to the stadium, the expansive Bois de Vincennes serves as a peaceful haven for those seeking to unwind from the Olympic fervor. Its picturesque pathways, tranquil bodies of water, and lush flora present an opportunity to savor the charm of Paris and explore its offerings beyond the adrenaline-fueled matches.

In essence, Stade Yves-du-Manoir is more than a mere sports facility; it embodies a legacy of athletic distinction and the pulsating heart of Parisian culture. The enthralling hockey events, set against both a historical edifice and the serene Bois de Vincennes, promise an experience that will linger in memory long after the 2024 Olympic Games have concluded.

Paris La Défense Arena

Situated on the outskirts of the bustling city center, nestled within Nanterre, stands the imposing Paris La Défense Arena, which boasts a seating capacity of 40,000. For the 2024 Olympic Games, this monumental structure will be repurposed as a sanctuary of aquatic prowess. The arena will feature an extraordinary exhibition of athleticism as competitors vie for glory in swimming, water polo, and para swimming events within this cutting-edge facility. Envision the arena alive with the palpable excitement as the world's premier swimmers converge upon a specially constructed, Olympic-grade, temporary pool for the Games. Spectators will be enthralled by the sheer velocity and exactitude displayed in the solo competitions, as well as the intricate teamwork seen in the relay races, all amplified by the fervor of an engaged audience. In addition to the individual and relay swim events, the Paris La Défense Arena will also be the stage for the exhilarating game of water polo. Teams will engage in a rigorous display of aquatic agility and strategic finesse, akin to an underwater dance, demanding superior physicality, collaboration, and strategic acumen. The audience's reactions will ebb and flow with the tempo of the matches, contributing to a memorable experience.

When the Olympic Games conclude, the venue will be reconfigured to accommodate the Paralympic Games' para swimming contests. The extraordinary talents and steadfast resolve of these para-athletes will be on full display as they partake in a variety of swimming challenges. Their perseverance and outstanding skills are set to inspire and captivate all who bear witness to their pursuit of Paralympic triumph.

Post-Games, the temporary pool will be deconstructed and moved to Saint-Denis, in line with the initial plans for the swimming facilities. This approach not only reflects a commitment to sustainability and judicious use of resources but also upholds the enduring spirit of the Games and promotes the future of aquatic sports in the area.

Thus, the Paris La Défense Arena will elevate beyond its temporary function as a sports facility. It will become an emblem of sporting prowess, inclusivity, and environmental stewardship. The enthralling aquatic performances across various disciplines during the Paris 2024 Games are set to offer a truly singular and memorable spectacle.

Aquatics Centre

Situated in Saint-Denis (93), adjacent to the renowned Stade de France, the Olympic Aquatics Centre embodies Paris' dedication to hosting premier sporting competitions. This facility, the only permanent structure erected exclusively for the Paris 2024 Games, falls under the governance of the Metropole du Grand Paris, representing a united effort to highlight the city's sports excellence on an international platform. The center is a vibrant nexus for three enthralling aquatic disciplines: artistic swimming, diving, and water polo. Equipped with cutting-edge amenities and strategically placed, it offers an ideal backdrop for competitors to exhibit their aquatic prowess.

In artistic swimming, teams will enchant spectators with their coordinated movements and creative expression, delivering performances marked by extraordinary precision and sophistication. The diving events promise to challenge the limits of athleticism as competitors execute complex aerial maneuvers with poise and precision. Water polo, known for its intense and strategic gameplay, will display the participants' power, tactical acumen, and collective effort as they battle for supremacy in the water.

The Aquatics Centre features an impressive spectator capacity, enabling a global audience to observe these aquatic marvels firsthand. The venue, with its contemporary facilities and elite infrastructure, ensures a lasting and engaging experience for everyone present. As the epicenter of aquatic competitions for the Paris 2024 Olympics, the Aquatics Centre is set to make an indelible mark on all who attend.

Stade de France

Towering over Saint-Denis (93), the Stade de France is renowned as the nation's most expansive stadium, erected initially for the 1998 Football World Cup. By 2024, it seamlessly assumes the esteemed position of the Olympic Stadium for the Paris Games, reflecting France's athletic zeal and rich cultural history. Since its debut, the Stade de France has emerged as the preferred site for numerous prominent sporting occasions. It played host to the World Athletics Championships in 2003, the Rugby World Cup in 2007, and the Euro 2016 Football Championship, marking significant chapters in sports history by welcoming a global assembly of athletes and enthusiasts.

The Stade de France transcends its role as a mere venue for sporting events; it stands as a paragon of distinction and a monument to solidarity. Its dynamic structure and elite amenities enable it to also be a top-tier concert destination, attracting preeminent performers from France and beyond annually. In anticipation of 2024, the Stade de France is set to be the focal point for a captivating array of Olympic events, including track and field, rugby, and para athletics. Its expansive seating capacity promises to deliver an intense spectator experience, ensuring every second is etched in memory. Positioned as the pulsating core of Olympic track and field, the Stade de France is prepared to usher in the global community and exalt the pinnacle of human athletic prowess on the most illustrious platform.

Le Bourget Sport Climbing Venue

In an audacious effort to inject creativity and variety into the Olympic Games, the Paris 2024 organizers are including the dynamic discipline of climbing for its notable second showing at the Olympics. This move highlights the Games' dedication to exploring new frontiers and expanding the limits of competitive sports. The core of this pioneering endeavor is the Le Bourget Sport Climbing Venue, which is set to become a hub of enthusiasm and exploration for both competitors and fans. Situated in the lively Seine-Saint-Denis area, this cutting-edge complex is designed not just as a stage for Olympic achievement but also as a contributor to the community's enduring benefit. The facility features five climbing structures, each thoughtfully crafted to offer a versatile and demanding environment for the athletes. Included in these is an indoor wall that provides a space for athletes to prepare and get in the zone before their events. The outdoor section showcases four walls, with three allocated for the sport climbing disciplines—speed, bouldering, and lead combined—and one additional wall for warming up, ensuring competitors are at their peak before they confront their competitive goals.

The Le Bourget venue's indoor amenities are set to fulfill a critical need within the Seine-Saint-Denis locale by addressing the scarcity of proper sports infrastructure. In doing so, Paris 2024 aims to motivate the youth to chase their sports ambitions and cultivate a commitment to fitness and well-being. As the sport of climbing asserts its presence at the Olympics once more, the Le Bourget Sport Climbing Venue symbolizes the ethos of progress and inclusiveness that propels Paris 2024. The towering structures and the limitless opportunities they present beckon athletes to strive upward and enable onlookers to experience the essence of human ambition and resolve.

North Paris Arena

Paris 2024 has revealed the transformation of the Villepinte exhibition center into the magnificent North Paris Arena, a sports complex designed to revolutionize the Olympic experience. Boasting a cutting-edge design and extensive seating, this adaptable arena is set to become a hub of athletic excellence and thrilling spectacles throughout the Olympic Games.

The North Paris Arena spans nine generous halls, showcasing France's dedication to facilitating premier sporting occasions. As the nation's most extensive exhibition space, it provides a versatile backdrop for a multitude of Olympic sports, including the fervor of boxing, the meticulousness of the modern pentathlon, and the excitement of sitting volleyball. Located in the core of Seine-Saint-Denis, Villepinte is the perfect site for this significant arena, providing easy access for the throngs of fans keen to experience the competition up close. The North Paris Arena's strategic location and spaciousness ensure that enthusiasts from all over can gather to embrace the Olympic ethos. As a key venue for Paris 2024, the North Paris Arena captures the ideals of inclusion and fellowship inherent in the Olympic tradition. Its adaptable structure and lively ambiance encourage athletes, fans, and guests to partake in the exhilaration of Olympic rivalry and the shared joy that surpasses cultural and geographical divides. With the North Paris Arena at its heart, Paris 2024 is preparing for an extraordinary homage to sportsmanship, companionship, and the profound ability of sports to motivate and elevate. As the global community converges on Villepinte, the anticipation builds for the memorable experiences that will unfold in the esteemed confines of this iconic sports facility.

Vaires-sur-Marne Nautical Stadium

Tucked within the charming terrain of Seine-et-Marne (77), the Vaires-sur-Marne Nautical Stadium emerges as a pinnacle of sportsmanship, inviting athletes worldwide to its immaculate waterways. Since its opening in June 2019, this modern facility has distinguished itself as a top venue for Olympic and Paralympic canoe-kayak and rowing competitions, aligning with revered sites such as Beijing and Sydney.

As one of a mere trio of locations globally capable of hosting events of such caliber, the Nautical Stadium captures the essence of water sports and competitive drive. Its expansive amenities harmoniously meld the allure of nature with the latest in sports technology, offering competitors an unmatched platform to demonstrate their abilities and chase Olympic dreams. The Vaires-sur-Marne Nautical Stadium accommodates a variety of water sports, from the high-octane rush of canoe sprints to the strategic elegance of rowing, including disciplines like canoe slalom, para canoe, and para rowing. These events play out on tranquil waters, setting the stage for the creation of champions and enduring sports legacies. More than just a stage for sporting feats, the Nautical Stadium symbolizes solidarity and inclusiveness, embracing athletes across all skill levels to partake in global competition. Its dedication to accessibility and top-tier standards ensures that the Olympic and Paralympic Games held in Vaires-sur-Marne epitomize a celebration of diversity, perseverance, and the limitless capabilities of the human spirit.

With Paris 2024 on the horizon, anticipation builds for the extraordinary events that will transpire on the glistening expanse of the Vaires-sur-Marne Nautical Stadium. In the heart of Seine-et-Marne, competitors and fans will converge to be part of history in progress and to savor the enchantment of the Olympic Games in their full splendor.

Château de Versailles

Immersed in the rich tapestry of France's illustrious past, the Château de Versailles emerges as an enduring emblem of the country's artistic and cultural heritage. Its impressive exterior and vast estate have consistently been admired as the epitome of royal refinement and architectural distinction. In an unprecedented partnership with the Paris Games of 2024, the Palace of Versailles is set to open its prestigious doors, inviting the global community to partake in an Olympic event of historic proportions. The Paris Games, set within the splendid surroundings of the Versailles estate, are poised to offer a spectacle that will captivate both live audiences and viewers worldwide. The palace's noble setting will host the fluid beauty of equestrian disciplines alongside the dynamic challenges of the modern pentathlon, providing a dignified platform for competitors to strive for Olympic success.

In a pioneering gesture, the Château de Versailles will also accommodate para equestrian competitions, reinforcing its dedication to diversity and barrier-free access. The participation of para athletes, exhibiting their prowess and resilience, will transform the palace into an icon of solidarity and inspiration, touching spectators across the globe with their remarkable accomplishments. As dusk embraces the golden pinnacles of Versailles, the Paris Games will unfold amid a display of unmatched opulence and allure. Within this historical and cultural setting, athletes from all corners of the world will gather to inscribe their achievements into the Olympic annals, their triumphs forever enshrined within the magnificent aura of the Château de Versailles.

Elancourt Hill

Situated at the summit of the region's tallest peak, 231 meters above sea level, Elancourt Hill stands out as a pinnacle of athletic prowess for the 2024 Paris Games. Nestled within the stunning vistas of Les Yvelines, the site offers a matchless perspective for spectators to experience the most captivating BMX competitions and performances ever presented in the Olympics. Choosing Elancourt as the BMX venue not only injects excitement into the Paris Games but also reinforces a vibrant center of sports within the area. Elancourt Hill, with its diverse ecosystems and untouched natural beauty, provides an ideal environment for competitors to challenge the limits of their abilities while maintaining a low environmental footprint. In alignment with sustainable practices and dedication to preserving the environment, no significant constructions will be erected at the location. The Olympic Mountain biking events will take advantage of pre-existing trails, with future routes incorporating 95% of these already-used paths. This considerate strategy not only safeguards the locale's aesthetic appeal but also contributes to a lasting heritage of trails for a variety of users, ranging from beginners to expert cyclists.

As BMX contestants navigate the paths of Elancourt Hill, they set out on an exhilarating quest marked by intense energy and exceptional skill. Amidst the grandeur of Les Yvelines, these intrepid competitors perform with elegance and exactitude, motivating people of all generations to celebrate the essence of adventure and rivalry. Within this natural amphitheater, the Paris Games at Elancourt Hill propel BMX to unprecedented levels, forging a memorable chapter in the annals of the Olympics.

Saint-Quentin-en-Yvelines BMX Stadium

Enclosed within the prestigious National Velodrome, the Saint-Quentin-en-Yvelines BMX Stadium rises as a pinnacle of cycling prowess for the 2024 Paris Games. Located in Montigny-le-Bretonneux (78), this cutting-edge venue features a custom-designed track engineered to test the mettle of elite BMX competitors. Through a fusion of creativity and technological advancement, the BMX stadium is seamlessly incorporated into the National Velodrome complex, providing a unique setting where BMX and track cycling events coalesce. As audiences assemble to observe the captivating BMX races, they are immersed in a dynamic showcase of velocity, dexterity, and heart-stopping excitement.

Conceived in tandem with the National Velodrome, the BMX course has been transformed and tailored to satisfy the rigorous demands of the Paris 2024 Games. Its enclosed construction guarantees consistent conditions for athletes to perform at their peak, while also offering a comfortable atmosphere for fans to revel in the thrill of BMX competitions. The Saint-Quentin-en-Yvelines BMX Stadium not only serves as a stage for world-class contests but also enriches the local community and cycling aficionados throughout France. Its openness to the general public and its capacity to cater to various proficiency levels promote a spirit of inclusiveness and participation, encouraging people of all backgrounds to experience the excitement of BMX cycling.

As the Paris Games take place in Montigny-le-Bretonneux, the Saint-Quentin-en-Yvelines BMX Stadium embodies the persistent essence of cycling distinction. In the sacred realm of the National Velodrome, competitors strive to transcend their limits, audiences exuberantly support their champions, and the enduring narrative of Paris 2024 is etched into the collective memory of all in attendance.

Saint-Quentin-en-Yvelines Vélodrome

The Saint-Quentin-en-Yvelines Vélodrome, a marvel of precise engineering and athletic distinction, shines as a hub of cycling supremacy, eagerly anticipating the arrival of elite track competitors for the prestigious Paris 2024 Games. Located in Montigny-le-Bretonneux and unveiled in 2014, this splendid construction captures the essence of sportsmanship and the collective pursuit of excellence. Purpose-built to accommodate leading competitions and to display the excitement of track cycling, the National Velodrome presents a top-tier setting for contenders to realize their Olympic and Paralympic aspirations. Its cutting-edge facilities and expertly designed track offer an optimal environment for athletes to challenge the limits of velocity and stamina.

Since its establishment, the velodrome has been the venue for notable events, solidifying its reputation as a top-tier destination for cycling. It has been the backdrop for the French track championships, World Championships, and European Championships, recording instances of victory and distinction that have secured its place in cycling lore. With the approach of the Paris 2024 Games, the Saint-Quentin-en-Yvelines Velodrome is prepared to once again leave an indelible mark on the international arena. Boasting superior amenities and a steadfast dedication to superiority, it is poised to be the focal point of track cycling during the Olympic and Paralympic Games, mesmerizing spectators with dynamic competitions and moments of unparalleled athletic prowess. Nestled in Montigny-le-Bretonneux, surrounded by the passionate applause of fans and the powerful resonance of competition, athletes from across the globe will gather to fulfill their ambitions and inscribe their achievements in the Olympic annals. As fate's wheels begin to turn, the Saint-Quentin-en-Yvelines Velodrome stands as a symbol of the perpetual flame of athleticism and the relentless quest for achievement.

Golf National

Tucked within the scenic vistas of France, Golf National stands as a distinguished establishment that represents the zenith of golfing prowess and the splendor of sportsmanship. Since it first opened its doors in 1991, this esteemed course has become synonymous with distinction, attracting the world's golfing elite to its revered courses and verdant putting surfaces. Hosting events like the esteemed French Open and the iconic Ryder Cup, Golf National has played a pivotal role in sporting lore, with its fairways and greens bearing witness to countless episodes of victory and celebration that have firmly imprinted on the chronicles of sports history. As Paris gears up for the honor of presenting the globe's most esteemed sporting competition in 2024, Golf National is primed to be the centerpiece for the Olympic games. Boasting impeccably maintained courses and facilities of the highest caliber, it presents an unmatched backdrop for the 120 competitors who will contend for Olympic distinction. Among its pair of 18-hole courses, "L'Albatros" is renowned for its demanding nature and intricate design, having welcomed major international contests, not least of which was the Ryder Cup in 2018.

Under the stewardship of the French Golf Federation, Golf National was thoughtfully crafted to become the heart of the national golf technical center and the honored setting for the French Open each year. An ambitious three-year project saw the transformation of a once level 139-hectare expanse into a golfer's utopia, complete with courses fit for championships and a 7-hole course designed for novices, thus accommodating players across the spectrum of ability. Golf National is also a proponent of sustainability, actively pursuing measures to bolster environmental management and conserve its valuable legacy. In partnership with the French Ministry of Ecology, Sustainable Development, and Energy, the teams at Golf National lead the way in eco-friendly endeavors, committed to maintaining the site as an exemplar of ecological guardianship.

With facilities that can host 32,720 spectators, including 2,720 in seating and 30,000 standing, Golf National is equipped to usher in both athletes and spectators to experience the apex of golfing achievement and the essence of the Olympic ethos. As the crème de la crème of the golfing world gather on its legendary courses, Golf National continues to embody a legacy of competitive excellence and the spirit of the Olympics.

Beyond Paris

As the 2024 Olympic Games pulsate through Paris, the fervor of the event radiates well beyond the French capital. This edition of the Games seeks to showcase France's cultural tapestry by igniting Olympic enthusiasm across its many locales, from dynamic cities to stunning natural vistas. The beautiful game of football, which reigns as the globe's most beloved sport, will be front and center in illustrious arenas within six French cities: Bordeaux, Nantes, Lyon, Saint-Etienne, Nice, and Marseille. These venues will provide fans throughout the nation the chance to partake in the Olympic football festivities, reflecting the widespread adoration for the sport in France.

Enthusiasts of handball and basketball can look forward to similar thrills. The handball tournament's climactic rounds will unfold in Lille, a city celebrated for its vibrant sports atmosphere. Concurrently, Lille will play host to basketball's qualifying matches, offering local supporters a preview of the Olympic competition before it culminates in Paris.

Extending even to France's overseas territories, the Games will break new ground as the Olympic surfing events are set to occur amidst the storied swells of Teahupo'o in Tahiti. This site, known for its stunning vistas and formidable waves, is set to provide an awe-inspiring setting for the sport. By dispersing the 2024 Games across various French regions and territories, the organizers underscore the event's commitment to inclusivity. This strategy enables not just Parisians but individuals from diverse communities throughout France and its territories to partake in this international sports festivity. The spread of Olympic excitement to multiple locations promises a truly cohesive and memorable experience for athletes, spectators, and the nation as a whole.

Pierre Mauroy Stadium

Situated in Villeneuve-d'Ascq, the Pierre Mauroy Stadium is a beacon of modern architecture and a hub for top-tier sports. Erected in 2012, this adaptable multi-purpose venue is the esteemed domain of LOSC, a top-tier French football team. Its importance, however, extends beyond just football, providing the Hauts de France area and the dynamic city of Lille with a multifaceted event space. The stadium's eye-catching structure combines beauty with practicality. Featuring a retractable roof, it can convert from an alfresco setting to a covered enclosure within 30 minutes, accommodating a diverse range of cultural and sports activities year-round. This architectural wonder has hosted major international events in various sports, including the Davis Cup tennis finals and the Euro 2016 Football Championship.

The Pierre Mauroy Stadium has also been the stage for legendary concerts by international stars such as Rihanna, Johnny Hallyday, and Depeche Mode, reinforcing its role as a hub of culture. Looking forward to the Paris 2024 Olympics, the stadium is set to host the handball competitions, offering a dynamic atmosphere with its 27,000-seat capacity as competitors chase Olympic triumph. The legacy of Pierre Mauroy Stadium will persist as a cutting-edge venue, enriching the Lille community with its dynamic capabilities. Whether it's international sports competitions or enthralling concerts, this architectural gem remains a pillar of cultural and athletic distinction in France's lively scene.

La Beaujoire Stadium

La Beaujoire Stadium is a monument to sporting achievement in the city of Nantes. Since 1984, this emblematic structure has been the epicenter of football for FC Nantes fans, celebrating four decades of sporting history. As it prepares to host Olympic events for the first time, La Beaujoire looks to add a new layer to its rich narrative. With its unique curved architecture, La Beaujoire represents more than just a stadium—it embodies local pride and enthusiasm. Known for its vibrant atmosphere, the stadium underwent extensive renovations in 1998 to accommodate the FIFA World Cup, thereby cementing its place as a leading sports venue in France.

La Beaujoire has been the setting for numerous unforgettable football moments, from the passionate chants of FC Nantes supporters to the fervent energy of international contests. Its storied past speaks to the unifying power of sports, bringing together fans from diverse backgrounds. As the Olympic Games approach, La Beaujoire invites participants and fans to become part of its illustrious history. With a capacity of 37,473, the stadium is primed to host an event that will captivate audiences worldwide. La Beaujoire Stadium continues to be a timeless homage to the unifying and inspirational nature of sports. As the Games proceed on its sacred grounds, it will blend the echoes of historic cheers with the excitement of future achievements, ensuring the stadium's legacy endures for future generations.

Châteauroux Shooting Centre

The serene Châteauroux landscape is home to the CNTS Shooting Centre, a sanctuary of sharpshooting prowess. Opened by the French Shooting Federation in 2018, this modern facility has become a gathering place for international marksmen to demonstrate their shooting expertise. With Paris set to host the 2024 Olympics, the Châteauroux Shooting Centre is poised to welcome 340 Olympic and 160 Paralympic athletes for the shooting competitions. Its extensive and sophisticated features make it one of the premier shooting venues in Europe, offering athletes a top-tier platform to excel. The center includes several ranges capable of accommodating all Olympic shooting disciplines. The addition of a specialized "finals" building in 2022 enhances the venue's capacity to host international pistol and rifle finals, providing an unmatched viewing experience for both competitors and spectators.

During the Paris 2024 Games, the finals building will resonate with the sounds of competition as athletes contend for Olympic and Paralympic medals. In the backdrop of this advanced facility, moments of victory and perseverance will be on full display, epitomizing the pinnacle of shooting sports. The Châteauroux Shooting Centre stands as a monument to the dedication to excellence and competitive spirit. As athletes take their shots and audiences watch with bated breath, the stage is set for a display of skill, focus, and unwavering precision at the Châteauroux Shooting Centre.

Lyon Stadium

Lyon Stadium emerges as a paragon of contemporary design and environmental consciousness, reflecting France's dedication to innovation and ecological care. As the home of Olympique Lyonnais, this versatile venue is the epitome of state-of-the-art architecture combined with green initiatives, making it an ideal location for the 2024 Olympic Games.

As France's third-largest stadium, Lyon Stadium boasts ample space to host an international audience. Its modern and elegant design not only sets the scene for athletic events but also symbolizes progress and visionary aspirations. Lyon Stadium is distinguished by its commitment to sustainability. Its commitment to reducing its ecological footprint is evident through its use of 100% renewable energy, partially supplied by solar panels on its roof. This environmentally friendly approach not only cuts down on carbon emissions but also paves the way for future sports facilities to adopt similar practices. Beyond its athletic functions, Lyon Stadium has been the venue for several major events, affirming its position as a top entertainment destination. From the Euro 2016 semi-finals to the 2018 Europa League final, the stadium has been the backdrop for celebrations of regional and international significance.

Moreover, Lyon Stadium has hosted concerts by world-renowned musicians, enhancing its cultural appeal. With its advanced amenities and eco-friendly focus, Lyon Stadium continues to enchant audiences and draw admiration for its harmonious integration of sports, entertainment, and environmental conscientiousness. As the global community gathers in Lyon for the 2024 Olympic Games, Lyon Stadium is prepared to add another chapter to its distinguished history. With its ethos of sustainability and modernity, it stands as a shining example of how sports venues can embrace the future while respecting the heritage of the past.

Geoffroy-Guichard Stadium

Geoffroy-Guichard Stadium, situated at the core of France, is an esteemed landmark that embodies the spirit and history of football. Since its establishment in 1931, the arena, lovingly dubbed the "Chaudron," has been a magnet for sport enthusiasts, hosting numerous unforgettable and significant events. Through the years, the stadium has seen extensive updates to improve its infrastructure and modernize its facilities, ensuring it meets modern sporting standards. Presently, it exemplifies a contemporary sports arena, offering advanced features and exceptional experiences for spectators.

As the proud home of the AS Saint-Etienne football team, Geoffroy-Guichard Stadium has welcomed various high-profile sports tournaments, reinforcing its role as a pivotal sports venue in France. It has been the center of action for the Euro 1984 Football Championship and the 1998 Football World Cup, among others. In addition to football, the stadium has been a venue for other events, like the 2007 Rugby World Cup and the Euro 2016 Football Championship, each adding to its rich history and solidifying its reputation as a sacred place for athletic contests. Despite its historical significance, Geoffroy-Guichard Stadium remains a lively and engaging venue, resonating with the enthusiasm of fans and the excellence of sportsmanship. It continues to draw in and inspire visitors with its blend of contemporary features and classic allure. As the stadium gears up to host the Olympic tournament, it is poised to offer a memorable experience that is rich in tradition, excitement, and the sheer joy of the beautiful game.

Bordeaux Stadium

Bordeaux Stadium is a marvel of architectural innovation and environmental commitment, preparing to shine once more in 2024 as it welcomes the world to Bordeaux for the Olympic Games. Located in the picturesque capital of the Gironde Region, Bordeaux Stadium impresses with its design, inspired by the Landes forest, and its facade adorned with iconic columns that reflect the surrounding natural beauty.

From the outset, Bordeaux Stadium was designed with sustainability in mind, featuring solar panels and other eco-friendly initiatives that exemplify responsible construction and serve as a model for future projects. Since opening, it has been the home ground for the Girondins de Bordeaux football club and has hosted a variety of sporting and cultural events, becoming a hub for entertainment and sports in the region.

As it prepares for the Paris 2024 Games, Bordeaux Stadium represents a fusion of unity, innovation, and the timeless spirit of competition. It promises a remarkable experience through its blend of spectacle and sustainability.

Nice Stadium

Nice Stadium, perched by the Mediterranean, is a showcase of modernity and eco-friendly design, set to host Olympic football matches in 2024. The home of OGC Nice, this versatile stadium is not only a sports venue but also houses the National Sports Museum, attracting numerous visitors each year. With a design that features solar panels and rainwater collection, Nice Stadium is a leader in sustainable architecture. It has hosted significant events, such as the Euro 2016 Football Championship, and can accommodate thousands of spectators, offering an electrifying atmosphere for fans.

As Nice Stadium gets ready for the Paris 2024 Games, it stands as a symbol of the captivating power of sport and the potential of green design. It promises an extraordinary experience that will leave lasting impressions on all who visit.

Marseille Stadium

Marseille Stadium, nestled in the bustling city of Marseille, is set to host the Olympic tournament in 2024. As France's second-largest stadium, it is a beacon of sporting prowess and a place of cultural importance. Constructed in 1937 and recently modernized in 2014, the stadium, with its distinctive roof and curved stands, provides an exceptional environment for spectators. It has been the venue for various world-class football and rugby events and is the home of Olympique de Marseille.

As Marseille readies itself to display its football heritage to the world during the Paris 2024 Games, Stade Vélodrome stands as a monument to the city's sporting legacy and dedication to excellence. It offers a blend of football history and modern comforts, ensuring an unforgettable experience for athletes and fans gathered to honor the universal spirit of sport.

Marseille Marina

As the 2024 Paris Olympics chart a course for the Mediterranean, Marseille is the evident host for the esteemed sailing competitions. Nestled in the heart of the Mediterranean's blue waters, Marseille is celebrated for its superb sailing conditions and a rich seafaring tradition, providing an ideal setting for this captivating contest. Marseille is distinguished for its proficiency in staging maritime events of global significance, and its Marina is a testament to sailing excellence. In anticipation of the 2024 Paris Games, Marseille has diligently prepared the Roucas-Blanc Marina, ensuring it is a venue befitting the splendor of the Olympics. The Marina has been meticulously upgraded, with about 7,000 square meters of indoor space and a reconfiguration of roughly 17,000 square meters of outdoor areas, all to adhere to the demanding expectations of the Olympic contests.

The Marseille Marina, with its cutting-edge facilities and scenic locale, promises competitors and fans an exceptional encounter where athletic endeavor meets natural beauty. As competitors sail through the Mediterranean's crystal-clear waters, they will encounter the distinctive allure and warm welcome of Marseille, a city with a legacy intertwined with nautical distinction. Embracing the Olympic spirit of unity and athletic excellence, the Marseille Marina is poised to host the global community, merging the enduring charm of sailing with the thrill of the Olympic Games, forging unforgettable moments.

Teahupo'o

Continuously striving for groundbreaking achievements and extraordinary athletic performances, the Paris 2024 Olympics will showcase four new and exciting sports, including surfing, to captivate a global audience. The event planners have carefully selected exceptional venues that enhance the thrill of these dynamic sports.

Surfing aficionados and competitors will be mesmerized by the stunning scenes at Teahupo'o, Tahiti. Here, surfers will tackle the legendary Teahupo'o wave, famous for its formidable power and stunning aesthetics. Chosen for its unmatched beauty and optimal surfing conditions, Teahupo'o is set to host a memorable and electrifying competition. Marking its second Olympic appearance after its introduction in Tokyo 2021, surfing has found a fitting arena in the illustrious Teahupo'o waters. Celebrated by the surfing community for its captivating charm and demanding nature, this emblematic wave captures the very heart of surfing and provides the backdrop for an extraordinary Olympic event.

The Paris 2024 organizers are dedicated to maintaining Teahupo'o's unspoiled natural beauty, emphasizing that this cherished location is preserved for future generations. By prioritizing sustainability, they plan to implement strategies that protect the island's unique environment, allowing competitors to perform in sync with the natural world. As elite surfers gather at Teahupo'o, they will pursue excellence amid the wild splendor of Tahiti. With each wave mastered and each technique performed with finesse, Teahupo'o will stand as a testament to the resilience of the human spirit and the enduring heritage of Olympic surfing.

Spectator etiquette and guidelines

As observers, we contribute significantly to the fabric of sporting spectacles, infusing the competitive atmosphere with our shared passion and excitement. However, with this privilege comes the duty to maintain decorum, ensuring a fully enjoyable experience for all attendees. Whether we are supporting our cherished competitors or observing monumental moments, it is crucial that we adhere to the expected standards of conduct to foster a welcoming and respectful atmosphere.

This manual is designed to provide you with the essential understanding and resources needed to support competitors fervently, yet with the dignity and reverence appropriate for such a distinguished occasion. Adherence to these instructions will guarantee that your participation augments the ambience and aids in creating the memorable moments that the 2024 Games strive to offer.

Enhancing Your Sporting Experience

Experiencing a live sports event is a thrilling affair, offering a chance to witness remarkable athletic prowess and join in the shared enthusiasm of like-minded supporters. Nonetheless, it's crucial for attendees to behave in a way that shows consideration for the competitors, officials, and fellow audience members, fostering a pleasant and enjoyable environment for everyone. In this discussion, we explore the nuances of proper spectator behavior and provide detailed advice to help you fully enjoy your sports event while maintaining the principles of fair play and courtesy.

Courtesy towards Athletes and Officials:
- Support your preferred athletes with vigor, but steer clear of negative comments or actions aimed at the opposition or their supporters.
- Refrain from jeering, taunting, or causing disturbances that could distract or dishearten the athletes or officials.
- Accept the rulings of referees, judges, and officials with grace, recognizing their role in promoting fairness and preserving the sport's integrity.

Mindfulness of Other Spectators:
- Be considerate of others' space and make sure not to block their view.
- Maintain a reasonable volume when talking or cheering to not disrupt those seated nearby.
- Avoid remaining on your feet too long, especially if it means obstructing the view for those behind you.
- When accompanied by young ones, instill in them the value of courteous conduct and supervise them to prevent disturbances to others.

Compliance with Venue Rules:
- Acquaint yourself with the venue's specific policies, including banned items, smoking zones, and allocated seating areas.
- Heed the directives of venue staff and security to keep a secure and orderly atmosphere for all present.
- Discard litter appropriately, using the bins and recycling options available.

Sensible Consumption of Refreshments:
- Partake in snacks and drinks judiciously, being conscious of any spills or clutter that could bother other attendees.
- Limit alcohol intake to prevent disruptive behavior that could spoil the event for you and others.

Positive Team Support:
- Show your team or athlete support with enthusiasm and a positive outlook, contributing to an energetic and engaging ambiance.
- Eschew negative chants, actions, or banners aimed at rival teams or their players to avoid raising tensions and creating a hostile atmosphere.

Awareness of Safety and Security:
- Stay alert and report any unusual or concerning activities to the venue's staff or security.
- Know where emergency exits are and understand evacuation protocols for a quick and coordinated reaction if needed.
- Be conscious of your environment and take measures to protect your possessions from theft or misplacement.

By observing these guidelines for spectator conduct, you not only increase your personal enjoyment of the sports event but also help cultivate a welcoming and inclusive environment for the competitors, officials, and your fellow enthusiasts. Let's unite in the celebration of sportsmanship and fellowship, ensuring every sports event is a memorable occasion for everyone involved.

Budgeting for the Games in Paris

Accommodation options: Hotels, hostels, and alternatives

Mob House: An Elegant Retreat Close to Olympic Excitement

Address:70 Rue des Rosiers, 93400 Saint-Ouen-sur-Seine, France

If you're on the hunt for a trendy and energetic base camp for your Paris Olympics adventure, Mob House is your go-to spot. This 4-star gem is perfectly positioned for a swift hop to the iconic Stade de France, a mere 23-minute subway trip away. Tucked away in a transformed warehouse, Mob House presents a stylish city retreat with an original vibe that's a welcome break from the bustle of Paris. Here, guests can kick back by the seasonal outdoor pool or lounge on the generous terrace. The in-house bar and eatery dish out organic eats and feature live DJ sessions, contributing to the lively mood. With 100 rooms decked out in simple sophistication, sporting neutral hues and touches of light wood, you can sink into tranquility after a thrilling day at the Olympics. The serene rooms are just the ticket for a good night's rest. For those after something different from the usual Parisian lodgings, Mob House stands out, situated near the historic Saint-Ouen flea market.

Starting at £282 a night (depending on when you book), Mob House's perks include an organic bar and restaurant, room service, a gym, options for pet owners, laundry facilities, and parking. Mob House hits the mark for fashion, convenience, and chill vibes for the 2024 Olympic Games crowd. Whether you're there for the easy access to Stade de France or to bask in the unforgettable Paris vibe, Mob House promises a stay that's nothing short of memorable.

Hôtel Cabane: A Quaint Parisian Haven for Olympic Enthusiasts
Address: 76 Rue Raymond Losserand, 75014 Paris, France

In search of a serene and delightful haven during the hustle of the 2024 Paris Olympics? Hôtel Cabane is your answer—a 4-star hidden gem in the city's core. Conveniently situated in the 14th arrondissement, Hôtel Cabane is a stone's throw from the Pernety Metro Station on Line 13, offering effortless travel throughout the city and swift access to the Olympic action, perfect for those heading to events at the nearby Paris Expo.

For those passionate about sports, the hotel's location is a dream come true, especially for handball, volleyball, and table tennis aficionados, with the Paris Expo venue a mere half-hour walk away. If it's a peaceful sanctuary you're after, Hôtel Cabane's tranquil garden and inviting rooms, echoing the charm of a mountain lodge, are sure to please.

Kick off your morning with a sumptuous breakfast of local fare, and cap off your Olympic days at the hotel's welcoming bar. With prices starting at £215 per night (availability dependent on dates), Hôtel Cabane's offerings include a bar, breakfast with locally sourced ingredients, a garden terrace, free WiFi, accommodations for pets, and laundry facilities. For those attending the Olympics, Hôtel Cabane promises a comfortable and quaint Parisian experience, perfectly placed for avid sports fans and a quiet respite from the Olympic buzz.

Plaza Tour Eiffel: Olympic Thrills with an Iconic Parisian Backdrop
Address: 32 Rue Greuze, 75016 Paris, France

Immerse yourself in the enchantment of the 2024 Olympics with a stay at the Plaza Tour Eiffel. Fresh from a makeover, this 4-star gem stands in the shadow of the majestic Eiffel Tower, offering a prime spot for all the action.

Why pick Plaza Tour Eiffel? Its prime position is a game-changer. Nestled just a stone's throw from the Seine, with the Eiffel Tower and Jardins du Trocadero as its neighbors, you're in the heart of the excitement, with a front-row seat to the Games and a host of venues within easy reach. Imagine stepping out of the hotel to catch beach volleyball, judo, and wrestling at the nearby Champ de Mars Arena and Eiffel Tower Stadium. It's all right there, waiting for you. Dreaming of a room with a view? Consider upgrading for a vista that will take your breath away. Picture waking up every day of your Olympic adventure to the sight of the Eiffel Tower right outside your window. Step into any of the 41 rooms and let the soothing blend of gold and blue hues wrap you in luxury. Every space is designed to be your tranquil haven, a place to recharge after a day of Olympic thrills.

Let's talk about perks. Starting at £282 a night, with variations depending on your dates, you'll enjoy amenities like a restaurant, bar, room service, free WiFi, a fitness center, options for your furry friends, and laundry services. Choose the Plaza Tour Eiffel for an Olympic adventure that's as much about the stay as it is about the games. It's the intersection of convenience, luxury, and those postcard-worthy Eiffel Tower snapshots that will make your 2024 Olympics an affair to remember.

Hotel des Grands Voyageurs: A Nostalgic Parisian Escape During the Olympics
Address: 92 Rue de Vaugirard, 75006 Paris, France

Immerse yourself in the vibrant fusion of Olympic excitement and the allure of Paris at the newly opened Hotel des Grands Voyageurs. Boasting four stars and situated in the city's pulsing heart, this hotel is a top pick for visitors of the 2024 Olympic Games, delivering a mix of style, convenience, and a distinctive vibe. One standout feature of Hotel des Grands Voyageurs is its prime spot in the city. Just a stone's throw away from the Esplanade des Invalides, it's a breeze for guests to stroll over to the archery competitions and soak up the Olympic thrills.

The hotel's design transports guests to a bygone era of celebrated writers and cultural legends with its nostalgic, chic decor. The ambiance at Hotel des Grands Voyageurs is not just welcoming, but it also captures a time of classic sophistication. When it comes to dining, the hotel doesn't disappoint. Whether you're savoring a meal at the in-house restaurant or toasting with a craft cocktail from the well-supplied bar, your palate is in for a treat with every morsel and drop. Guests can expect contemporary amenities in their cozy rooms, including complimentary WiFi. The hotel's thoughtful services, like room service, laundry, a children's club, and parking (check for availability), are designed to make your visit as smooth and pleasant as possible.

Starting at £314 per night (availability may vary depending on the date), Hotel des Grands Voyageurs provides a host of features, including a restaurant, room service, a bar, free WiFi, a kids' club, pet accommodations, laundry, and parking options. For those searching for an accommodation that's both chic and handy during the Olympics, Hotel des Grands Voyageurs is an exceptional choice. It's not just about the prime location or the amenities; it's about the memorable stay you'll have while witnessing the 2024 Games.

TOO Hotel: Olympic Excitement Amidst Stunning Parisian Panoramas
Address: 65 Rue Bruneseau, 75013 Paris, France

Immerse yourself in the electric buzz of the 2024 Olympics, surrounded by the captivating Parisian skyline at TOO Hotel. Nestled in the lively 13th arrondissement, this 4-star avant-garde hotel boasts remarkable urban vistas and sits at the heart of the action for several Olympic showdowns. Why pick TOO Hotel? The views are a game-changer. Imagine savoring a meal in the sky-high restaurant, with the city's famous monuments unfolding before you—a truly mesmerizing scene to complement your Olympic journey.

Location-wise, TOO Hotel hits the bullseye. A brisk stroll lands you right at the Bercy Arena, a haven for enthusiasts of basketball, trampoline, and artistic gymnastics. Get ready to dive into the Olympic spirit without a hitch. The hotel's futuristic flair is like stepping into tomorrow. Its cutting-edge design and chic decor set the stage for a memorable stay during the Olympics. Picture yourself in a world where elegance meets innovation.

Culinary adventures await at the hotel's restaurant, where the art of fine dining meets the allure of the cityscape. Cap off a thrilling day at the Games with a celebratory drink at the bar, cherishing the moments that will turn into lifelong memories. Seeking a sanctuary?

TOO Hotel's wellness offerings, including a sauna, gym, and spa (availability permitting), provide the perfect retreat for both relaxation and keeping up with your fitness routine.

Here's the lowdown: Rooms start at £299 per night, varying with specific dates. TOO Hotel's amenities include a restaurant with a view, room service, a bar, free WiFi, laundry facilities, parking (space permitting), a sauna, a gym, and a spa (subject to availability). For those chasing a contemporary and opulent haven during the 2024 Olympics, TOO Hotel is a standout choice. With its awe-inspiring panoramas, prime positioning, and state-of-the-art facilities, it's set to deliver an Olympic experience that's as unforgettable as the Games themselves.

Generator Hostel: An Economical Hub for Olympic Enthusiasts

Address: 9-11 Pl. du Colonel Fabien, 75010 Paris, France
If you're on the hunt for a wallet-friendly yet stylish spot to kick off your Olympic adventure, Generator Hostel is your go-to place. Nestled in the lively eastern district of Paris, this hostel is a hub of friendliness and convenience, ideal for those looking to soak up the Olympic spirit without splurging too much. One of the top draws of Generator Hostel is its pocket-friendly prices. You can snag a room starting at only £47 a night, offering a thrifty option compared to standard hotels. This means you can save some cash while still enjoying a snug stay in the City of Light. The location of Generator Hostel is a huge plus, situated a stone's throw from the charming Canal St Martin and within a short stroll to the Gare du Nord station, making zipping around Paris a breeze. Whether you're off to catch the Olympic action or to visit the city's famed sights, the hostel's central spot is super handy for all sorts of excursions. The hostel buzzes with a lively vibe, perfect for connecting with other Olympic enthusiasts and forging new international friendships. Whether you're sharing tales in the shared spaces or sipping a beverage at the rooftop bar, Generator Hostel is all about fun encounters and memorable times.
Beyond the friendly atmosphere, Generator Hostel packs in all the must-haves to uplift your stay. With perks like the city-view rooftop bar, an underground club, free WiFi, laundry options, and a policy that welcomes pets, the hostel checks all the boxes for a relaxed and fun Parisian experience.
Plus, Generator Hostel is conveniently close to the Porte de la Chapelle Arena, the venue for badminton and rhythmic gymnastics, making it a breeze to get to the heart of the Olympic buzz.Room rates kick off at £47 per night (varying with specific dates), and you can enjoy amenities like a rooftop bar, an underground club, free WiFi, laundry facilities, and a pet-friendly approach. For those who prize both their social life and their wallets, Generator Hostel is an unbeatable choice for the 2024 Olympic Games. It's a place that

promises a memorable stay with its budget-friendliness, prime location, vibrant social scene, and all the essentials you need, welcoming guests from across the globe to join in the excitement.

Hotel Dame des Arts

Address: 4 Rue Danton, 75006 Paris, France

Experience the ultimate indulgence at Hotel Dame des Arts during the 2024 Olympic Games! This hotel is a haven of luxury, offering sweeping views of the city, top-notch facilities, and a location that's just perfect for diving into the Olympic excitement and city's charm. What really makes Hotel Dame des Arts stand out is its breathtaking views—imagine sipping a drink at the rooftop bar or unwinding on your own private balcony, with Paris spread out before you.

The hotel wraps you in elegance, right down to its unique scent, ensuring your stay is nothing short of magnificent. Comfort is king here, with every detail crafted for your pleasure. Getting around is a breeze, thanks to the nearby Saint-Michel Notre-Dame Metro station, making it a snap to get to all the Olympic action. And when you need a moment to relax, the hotel's spa, sauna, steam room, and gym are there to pamper you. You've got everything you need on-site, including dining, a bar, free WiFi, pet-friendly vibes, laundry service, and even a kids' club, depending on availability.

Room rates for the Olympic period begin at £460 a night, and they can vary, so keep that in mind. With amenities like a rooftop bar, restaurant, wellness center, free WiFi, pet accommodations, laundry facilities, and a kids' club (availability permitting), Hotel Dame des Arts is the epitome of comfort, convenience, and luxury for an unforgettable Olympic experience.

Hotel Le Versailles

Address: 7 Rue Sainte-Anne, 78000 Versailles, France

Hotel Le Versailles is ideally situated just a leisurely walk away from the Château de Versailles, making it super easy to get to the Olympic festivities happening right there. If you're looking for a place to crash, they've got you covered with snug rooms that come with all the modern perks like free Wi-Fi, flat-screen TVs, and minibars. And if you're lucky, you might even snag a room with an amazing view of the Château de Versailles itself. Plus, you can kick off your day with a hearty buffet breakfast in a bright and airy dining area.

When it comes to cost, you're looking at spending somewhere between €150 and €250 a night at Hotel Le Versailles. The price tag will change up a bit depending on what kind of room you pick and when you're planning to stay. So, whether you're here to cheer on the athletes at the Château de Versailles or just to soak in the local sights, Hotel Le Versailles is a solid pick for a comfy and handy spot to stay during the Olympic buzz.

Trianon Palace Versailles, A Waldorf Astoria Hotel

Address: 1 Bd de la Reine, 78000 Versailles, France

Nestled close to the regal Palace of Versailles and surrounded by sweeping gardens, the Trianon Palace Versailles provides a peaceful haven, perfect for those visiting for the Olympic happenings at the château. This hotel is home to roomy guest rooms and suites, each one tastefully adorned with classy furnishings for a touch of luxury. Food lovers can savor the exquisite dishes at the Michelin-starred Gordon Ramsay au Trianon restaurant, and those looking to unwind will find bliss at the Guerlain Spa. With added perks like a fitness center, an indoor pool, and tennis courts, guests are sure to enjoy a comprehensive and delightful stay.

As for the cost, a typical night's stay in a standard room at the Trianon Palace Versailles typically falls between €300 and €600, while the more opulent suites might go over €1000. Keep in mind, prices can shift with the seasons and depending on how full the hotel is. Whether you're in search of a quiet spot close to nature or a sumptuous retreat with top-notch dining and spa services, the Trianon Palace Versailles has a little something for everyone, ensuring your visit during the Olympic Games is one for the books.

Hotel Le Louis Versailles Château – MGallery

Address: 2 Bis Av. de Paris, 78000 Versailles, France

At the Hotel Le Louis Versailles Château – MGallery, you'll find a perfect mix of old-world elegance and contemporary comfort, just a stone's throw from the famed Château de Versailles. Each room is tastefully decorated and comes with all the essentials like air conditioning, facilities to make coffee or tea, and top-notch bedding to ensure a restful sleep. If you're looking to chill out, the hotel's cocktail bar is the ideal spot, or you can melt away stress in the sauna. Plus, there's a scrumptious buffet breakfast available if you're up for it, though it's a bit extra.

When it comes to cost, you're looking at a range of €200 to €350 per night to stay at this chic spot, but prices can swing a bit depending on when you book and the room you pick. So whether you're in town to soak up the history of Versailles or you're here for the excitement of the Olympic events, this hotel is a swanky choice for travelers who appreciate the finer things.

Hôtel des Lys

Address: 16 Rue Richaud, 78000 Versailles, France

Situated in the vibrant heart of Versailles, Hôtel des Lys is just a stone's throw away from the iconic Palace. Its superb location is perfect for visitors who are in town for the Olympic happenings at the château or keen on checking out the local sights. The hotel boasts quaint and cozy rooms, each with a touch of classic French elegance, ensuring a snug haven for travelers. Guests can expect up-to-date facilities such as flat-screen TVs, free Wi-Fi, and snug bedding for a restful night's sleep. Plus, there's a continental breakfast available every morning in the welcoming breakfast area to kick-start your day.

When it comes to cost, a night at Hôtel des Lys is usually priced between €100 and €200, although this can vary depending on room size and the season. So, whether you're here for the thrill of the Olympics or to soak in Versailles' storied past and vibrant culture, Hôtel des Lys presents a delightful and handy stay without breaking the bank.

The Peninsula Paris

Address: 19 Av. Kléber, 75116 Paris, France

Indulge in the opulence of The Peninsula Paris, a 5-star haven in the city's core. This historic edifice, now exquisitely restored, promises an extraordinary stay for the discerning guest during the Olympic festivities. Consider making The Peninsula Paris your home away from home for its prime position on Avenue Kleber, right at the pulse of Paris. This hotel stands just a stone's throw from the majestic Arc de Triomphe and a multitude of Olympic venues, nestled in the city's lively core. It marries sleek modernity with classic French elegance, offering an experience steeped in the luxurious essence of Paris. The walls of The Peninsula are adorned with a vast art collection, over 1,379 pieces, enveloping guests in a sophisticated cultural milieu. The service at The Peninsula

Paris is second to none, with a tailored approach to hospitality that aims to fulfill your every desire, making every visit uniquely memorable. Culinary adventures await at the hotel's Michelin-starred eateries, while the rooftop bar presents sweeping views of the cityscape. For moments of leisure, choose from the refined settings for afternoon tea or a cocktail. To relax and recharge, the hotel provides a full suite of amenities, including a spa, an indoor pool, saunas, steam rooms, and a state-of-the-art fitness center.

Bear in mind, the opulence of The Peninsula Paris comes with a significant price, positioning it as a destination for those in pursuit of high-end lodging for the 2024 Olympics. Given its fame, particularly during big events like the Olympics, it's wise to book early to ensure your spot at this prestigious hotel. For details and reservations, head to The Peninsula Paris website: (https://www.peninsula.com/en/paris/5-star-luxury-hotel-16th-arrondissement)

Four Seasons Hotel

Address: 31 Av. George V, 75008 Paris, France

Nestled in the Golden Triangle, the Four Seasons Hotel George V, Paris is a beacon of grandeur, offering an unparalleled stay for those attending the 2024 Olympics. It's renowned for its stunning views, gourmet dining experiences, and impeccable service, truly embodying the pinnacle of Parisian luxury for guests who expect nothing less than extraordinary during their Olympic visit.

Staying at the Four Seasons Hotel George V means you're right in the heart of the action on Avenue George V, just a stone's throw away from the excitement of the Olympics and the timeless beauty of Parisian hotspots like the Champs-Élysées. The hotel's Art Deco charm will sweep you off your feet, with elegant interiors and a signature scent that envelop you in sheer opulence. Imagine waking up to breathtaking views of Paris, with the Eiffel Tower in full sight from your room or balcony – it's part of what makes this place so magnetic.

For those with a taste for the finer things in life, the hotel's trio of Michelin-starred restaurants is a culinary playground where top-notch chefs serve up memorable feasts. When it's time to unwind, the sophisticated bars and lounges are the perfect spots to chill out or mingle. Here, every guest is a VIP, with services customized to your preferences, ensuring a stay that's nothing short of perfect. Beyond the exquisite rooms, the Four Seasons Hotel George V invites you to pamper yourself in its sumptuous spa, hit the gym in style, take a dip in the indoor pool, or find serenity in the peaceful courtyard – it's all about indulgence, wellness, and fun.

Just a heads-up, though: luxury like this does come with a price tag to match. And with the hotel's popularity, especially when big events are in town, make sure you book ahead. To plan your stay, head over to the Four Seasons Hotel George V website: [Four Seasons Paris](https://www.fourseasons.com/paris/). Remember, a little planning goes a long way!

The Mandarin Oriental

Address: 251 Rue Saint-Honoré, 75001 Paris, France

The Mandarin Oriental in Paris is a beacon of 5-star luxury, perfectly blending the city's historic charm with modern amenities. Nestled in the esteemed 1st arrondissement on the fashionable Rue Saint-Honoré, this exquisite hotel is a prime choice for those visiting the 2024 Olympics.

Why Choose the Mandarin Oriental in Paris:

Just a stone's throw from Place Vendôme and the iconic Louvre, the hotel is ideally positioned for easy access to Olympic events and the bustling Parisian scene. Its central locale is perfect for guests eager to discover the city's rich cultural offerings. The hotel boasts beautiful gardens, soaring ceilings, and sumptuous decor that hark back to Paris's opulent past. Yet, it's the infusion of sleek, modern design that truly sets the scene for a luxurious stay that honors tradition while embracing the present. Under the guidance of Chef Thierry Marx, the hotel's two Michelin-starred eateries promise an exceptional dining adventure, brimming with inventive dishes and exquisite flavors. The chic bar and charming patisserie complement the gastronomic journey.

The Mandarin Oriental is synonymous with personalized attention and care. Every detail of your visit is meticulously catered to, ensuring a stay that not only meets but surpasses your every expectation. Drawing on Eastern practices, the hotel's spa is a haven for those seeking peace and renewal. Guests can enjoy a variety of soothing treatments, relax in the serene ambiance, or keep up with their workout routine in the top-notch fitness center and inviting indoor pool.

Things to Consider:

- Premium Pricing: Reflecting its status as a top-tier establishment, the Mandarin Oriental's rates are on the higher end. Guests should anticipate paying more for the exceptional services and facilities on offer.
- Book Early: The hotel's allure, especially during high-profile events like the Olympics, means rooms can fill up fast. To ensure you get the accommodation you want, it's wise to reserve well in advance, as spaces are likely to be in high demand.

For an unforgettable experience of luxury and elegance at the 2024 Olympics, the Mandarin Oriental in Paris stands out as a premier choice. To learn more or to make a reservation, visit their website: [Mandarin Oriental, Paris](https://www.mandarinoriental.com/en/paris/place-vendome).

Shangri-La Hotel

Address: 10 Av. d'Iéna, 75116 Paris, France

Shangri-La Hotel, Paris is a sumptuous 5-star establishment nestled in the chic 16th arrondissement, marrying traditional French charm with contemporary finesse. Shangri-La Hotel Overlooks the Seine River with the Eiffel Tower in view, providing impressive vistas and convenient access to Olympic sites and landmarks.

This beautiful hotel occupies the erstwhile abode of Prince Roland Bonaparte, officially recognized as a historic French monument, offering a distinctive historical setting. It features high-end rooms and suites with fine decor, some boasting direct views of the Eiffel Tower. Home to multiple celebrated dining venues, including a Michelin-starred Cantonese restaurant and a rooftop bar with sweeping city views. Includes a high-end spa, an indoor pool, a fitness center, and an enchanting garden courtyard. Shangri-La Hotel is known for its tailored and meticulous service, ensuring a memorable and smooth experience.

Reflecting its luxury status, it is more expensive than other Parisian accommodations. Its desirable location and acclaim mean that rooms are quickly reserved, particularly during high-demand periods like the Olympics. Prompt reservation is advised. Proximity to Downtown: While well-connected, it's situated around 2.7 miles from the city center, possibly necessitating extra travel time for certain activities.

Hotel du Louvre, in The Unbound Collection by Hyatt:
Address: Pl. André Malraux, 75001 Paris, France

Located in the pulsating heart of Paris, mere steps from the legendary Louvre Museum and the idyllic Palais Royal gardens, Hotel du Louvre resides in the dynamic 1st arrondissement. Its central location ensures guests are within reach of Paris' major landmarks, cultural attractions, shopping areas, and Olympic venues.

Features:

- Grand Accommodations: Hotel du Louvre offers spacious and sophisticated guest rooms and suites, each designed to offer a harmonious blend of Parisian elegance and modern luxury. Guests can enjoy plush bedding, contemporary décor, and high-end amenities, including speedy internet, flat-screen televisions, minibars, and marble bathrooms stocked with lavish toiletries. Select rooms afford breathtaking views of the Louvre Museum, Opera Garnier, or Parisian streetscapes.
- Gastronomic Venues: The hotel features two exquisite dining options, each presenting the pinnacle of French culinary artistry. The Brasserie du Louvre provides a casual yet upscale setting for traditional French cuisine, while the chic Bar de l'Opera offers a selection of sophisticated cocktails, fine wines, and light fare.
- Fitness Facility: A fully equipped fitness center at Hotel du Louvre allows guests to keep up with their fitness regimen, offering modern workout equipment, cardio machines, and weights in a comfortable setting.
- Concierge Services: The hotel's expert concierge team is available around the clock to help with transportation, attraction tickets, dining reservations, and insider tips for exploring Paris. Whether planning Olympic activities or special occasions, the concierge is dedicated to creating a memorable stay.
- Event Venues: With flexible event spaces and modern meeting rooms, Hotel du Louvre is an excellent choice for hosting business events, weddings, and other gatherings. The event planning team is adept at tailoring events to meet guests' specific needs, ensuring a successful outcome.
- Rates: Accommodation rates at Hotel du Louvre typically range from €300 to €800 per night, with variations depending on room type, season, and booking availability. Special packages such as romantic escapes, family holidays, and

cultural experiences may be offered to enhance guests' stays with additional benefits and unique opportunities.

Hotel du Louvre, a member of The Unbound Collection by Hyatt, presents an unparalleled Parisian experience for discerning guests. With its luxurious rooms, exceptional dining, outstanding service, and prime location near renowned attractions, the hotel serves as an exquisite sanctuary for those looking to savor the enchantment of Paris during the 2024 Olympics.

Budget-Friendly Hotels (2-star):

Hotel Esmeralda
4 Rue Saint-Julien le Pauvre, 75005 Paris, France

Location: Tucked away in the vibrant Latin Quarter, Hotel Esmeralda stands on the scenic Seine River's edge, offering guests a historically-rich sanctuary amidst cultural splendor. Positioned on the time-honored Rue de la Huchette, this hotel is just a short stroll from iconic landmarks such as the Notre Dame Cathedral and the Sorbonne University, surrounded by a plethora of cafes, bistros, and bookstores. Its central location affords convenient access to Paris' Olympic venues and a myriad of cultural attractions and lively districts.

Amenities:
- Charming Guest Rooms: The hotel boasts quaint and distinctive rooms, each decorated with antique furnishings, visible wooden beams, and quintessential Parisian flair. These accommodations radiate comfort and hospitality, serving as a serene haven amidst the energetic Parisian streets. Modern conveniences such as complimentary Wi-Fi, flat-screen televisions, and private bathrooms with showers are standard in every room.
- Time-Honored Ambiance: Occupying a delightful 17th-century edifice, Hotel Esmeralda is a testament to classic Parisian style and history. The hotel invites guests to dive into an era past, with its spiral staircases,

hardwood railings, and preserved architectural elements. In the lobby, a snug lounge area awaits, where guests can unwind with literature or engage in conversation, reminiscent of an earlier time.
- Tailored Hospitality: The hotel prides itself on its dedicated team, committed to delivering bespoke service to ensure an unforgettable visit for each guest. Whether it's coordinating airport shuttles, booking dining experiences, or sharing local secrets for city exploration, the warm and expert staff at Hotel Esmeralda is readily available to fulfill any need and extend a hospitable welcome.
- Picturesque Vistas: Select rooms at Hotel Esmeralda present breathtaking views of the Seine River, Notre Dame Cathedral, or the historic Latin Quarter's avenues. Guests can begin their day with the inspiring sights of Paris' emblematic monuments and savor the city's charm from the solace of their room, enhancing the enchantment of their stay.
- Secluded Courtyard: The hotel is graced with a delightful courtyard, a serene spot for guests to relax and find repose. Whether starting the morning with a fresh brew or ending the day with a fine wine, the courtyard offers a quiet retreat from the city's commotion, providing a space for guests to refresh and revitalize.
- Pricing: The Hotel Esmeralda's rates typically span from €100 to €250 nightly, varying with room type, seasonality, and availability. The hotel presents reasonably priced lodging with exceptional value for those in search of a distinctive and genuine Parisian experience in the city's core.

Hotel Esmeralda is an idyllic fusion of historical allure, intimate guest rooms, and attentive service, nestled in one of Paris' most captivating quarters. With its prime site, scenic outlooks, and tranquil ambiance, the hotel stands as an ideal base for discovering the city's cultural jewels and Olympic venues during the Paris 2024 Games.

Hotel ibis Styles Paris République
Address: 9 Rue Léon Jouhaux, 75010 Paris, France

Location: Nestled in the dynamic République district within Paris' 11th arrondissement, the Hotel ibis Styles Paris République lies in a prime spot for those visiting to take in the Olympic festivities. Adjacent to the animated Place de la République, renowned for its array of cafes, boutiques, and historical importance, the hotel's central location ensures seamless access to various modes of public transport, including metro lines and bus routes, facilitating effortless navigation throughout Paris and to Olympic sites in and around the city.

Amenities:
- Contemporary Rooms: The Hotel ibis Styles Paris République boasts modern, chic guest rooms crafted for utmost comfort and convenience. Adorned with lively hues, current furniture, and essentials like flat-screen televisions, air conditioning, complimentary Wi-Fi, and snug bedding, the rooms offer a tranquil haven to unwind after an exhilarating day of Olympic events, amidst the city's lively atmosphere.
- Family-Oriented Accommodations: With an eye on accommodating families, the hotel provides family rooms and specific amenities for those traveling with children. The family-oriented spaces are generous and fully furnished to cater to their unique requirements, featuring interconnecting rooms, baby cribs, and extra bedding choices. The Hotel ibis Styles Paris République fosters a family-welcoming ambience, making it an ideal choice for a delightful Parisian stay during the Olympic Games.
- Complimentary Morning Meal: Each morning, guests are treated to a free breakfast at the Hotel ibis Styles Paris République. The breakfast spread includes an assortment of choices like oven-fresh pastries, assorted bread, cereal, yogurt, seasonal fruits, and warm drinks, offering a tasty and invigorating beginning to a day of city exploration or Olympic participation.
- Vibrant Surroundings: The République neighborhood, where the hotel is located, presents a spirited and engaging environment for guests to soak in Parisian life and culture. The area is dotted with a diverse blend of stores, eateries, cafes, and entertainment spots, allowing guests to dive into the local scene and relish the dynamic atmosphere. A short walk from the hotel, visitors can discover a wealth of activities along the verdant boulevards and nearby points of interest.

- Helpful Amenities: The Hotel ibis Styles Paris République provides a variety of helpful amenities to elevate the guest experience, including a 24-hour front desk, baggage storage, and assistance with tours. The hotel's dedicated and responsive staff are always available to help with queries

or requests, ensuring a smooth and pleasant Parisian sojourn.
- Pricing: The cost for a stay at the Hotel ibis Styles Paris République typically falls between €80 and €150 per night, varying with the type of room selected, the time of year, and booking availability. The hotel delivers reasonably priced lodging that doesn't compromise on comfort or convenience, making it an excellent choice for those seeking a central Parisian location.

The Hotel ibis Styles Paris République extends a warm welcome to those visiting for the vibrant République area and the thrill of the Paris 2024 Olympic Games. With its up-to-date accommodations, amenities suited for families, and an animated locale, the hotel is an ideal hub for experiencing the Olympic venues and the cultural offerings of the city.

Beyond the City Lights:

Île-de-France Charm

Waldorf Astoria Versailles - Trianon Palace

Address: 1 Bd de la Reine, 78000 Versailles, France

The Waldorf Astoria Versailles:
Positioned in the vibrant core of Versailles, a mere whisper away from the renowned Château de Versailles, The Waldorf Astoria Versailles presents a serene and opulent sanctuary encircled by the city's storied allure. Its strategic placement offers effortless entry to the Olympic equestrian and modern pentathlon events, while also allowing visitors to delve into Versailles' profound historical and cultural fabric. Accessibility to the Versailles-Château-Rive-Gauche train station further simplifies travel to Paris and additional Olympic sites throughout France.

Facilities:
- Sumptuous Lodgings: The hotel prides itself on its extravagant guest quarters, crafted to exude maximum comfort and sophistication. Each room and suite is adorned with elegant decor, lavish furnishings, and a host of premium comforts, including deluxe bedding, marble-clad bathrooms, state-of-the-art flat-screen TVs, well-stocked minibars, and complimentary internet access. Guests can bask in the grandeur of their accommodations while enjoying sweeping vistas of the gardens or the Château de Versailles from their own balconies or terraces.

- Gourmet Dining: The hotel's dining experiences are of regal caliber, featuring outstanding culinary offerings and flawless service. Patrons can relish in refined French dishes, the creations of celebrated chefs, within the hotel's flagship restaurant. The establishment emphasizes seasonal produce and avant-garde gastronomy. Moreover, the sophisticated bar and lounge serve as ideal locales for guests to relax with artisanal cocktails, select wines, and appetizing snacks in an elegant setting.
- Wellness and Leisure: Guests are invited to unwind within the hotel's sumptuous wellness amenities, which include a modern fitness center, an indoor pool, and a spa. A variety of soothing treatments and therapies, rooted in time-honored wellness practices, are available to encourage relaxation and holistic health. Whether it's a calming massage or a refreshing dip, the hotel's wellness haven is a place to let go of life's pressures and indulge in tranquility.
- Event Venues: This establishment is equipped with sophisticated event spaces and conference rooms, complete with advanced technology and bespoke services, making it an exemplary choice for business functions, matrimonial celebrations, and social events. Its picturesque surroundings and impeccable service render The Waldorf Astoria Versailles a memorable setting for any special occasion.
Impeccable Service: The hotel is celebrated for its iconic hospitality and meticulous attention to detail, offering guests a service that is second to none. The staff are devoted to fulfilling custom excursion arrangements, private tours, and special requests, ensuring each aspect of a guest's stay surpasses their anticipations and leaves indelible impressions.
- Rates: The Waldorf Astoria Versailles' room prices fluctuate based on the room selection, time of year, and availability, typically commencing from €500 to €1000 nightly for standard accommodations. Guests can take advantage of exclusive packages and promotions, including romantic escapes, spa retreats, and culinary journeys, enhancing the value and luxury of their visit.

At The Waldorf Astoria Versailles, guests are treated to an unmatched blend of timeless grace and contemporary luxury, set against the picturesque backdrop of Versailles. Whether in town for the Olympics, exploring historical sites, or seeking a lavish getaway, visitors are guaranteed an exceptional experience that will exceed all expectations.
Games.

B&B Le Logis Versaillais
28 Rue des États Généraux, 78000 Versailles, France

B&B Le Logis Versaillais is nestled in the scenic town of Versailles, mere moments from the renowned Palace of Versailles. This bed and breakfast is a cozy and convenient choice for visitors to the Paris 2024 Olympics, offering proximity to equestrian and modern pentathlon events, and easy access to Paris via public transport.

Features:
- Inviting Guest Rooms: The B&B presents a range of inviting guest rooms, each adorned with tasteful decor and outfitted with contemporary amenities for a restful stay. Options span from single to family rooms, all designed to serve as a comfortable haven following Olympic festivities.
- Artisanal Morning Fare: A homemade breakfast awaits guests each morning, featuring a variety of freshly baked goods, local jams, fruits, yogurt, and hot drinks, all crafted with locally sourced ingredients. The dining area or terrace offers a delightful ambiance for guests to enjoy their morning meal.
- Attentive Personal Service: The B&B's hospitable staff are committed to ensuring a pleasant stay, offering local insights, dining suggestions, help with travel plans, and assistance in obtaining Olympic event tickets. Their dedication to guest satisfaction contributes to an exceptional and memorable stay.
- Complimentary Wi-Fi Access: Guests can stay connected with complimentary high-speed Wi-Fi throughout the B&B, perfect for sharing Olympic moments or keeping up with work commitments.
- Prime Location: The B&B's location is ideal for guests wishing to visit the Palace of Versailles, with its proximity allowing for leisurely exploration. Public transport options nearby provide convenient travel to Paris and surrounding attractions.
- Pricing: Accommodation rates at B&B Le Logis Versaillais are variable, generally ranging from €80 to €150 per night, with fluctuations based on room size, occupancy, and the season. The B&B offers competitive rates and special deals, such as discounts for longer stays and early reservations, making it an attractive choice for those attending the Olympics.

Discover the warmth and charm of B&B Le Logis Versaillais during your Versailles visit for the Paris 2024 Olympics. With its cozy rooms, homemade breakfasts, and personalized attention, this bed and breakfast promises a welcoming and restful experience amidst the thrill of the Games.

Alternative Accommodations:

Use booking platforms like Booking.com or TripAdvisor to compare options.

Explore smaller boutique hotels for potentially more intimate and cost-effective options.

Food and dining options: Restaurants, cafes, and on-site options

Paris Region

Proximity: Stade de France (Athletics)

Bistrot de la Gare

1 Rue de Lyon, 75012 Paris, France

Tucked away in the bustling center of Paris, a mere whisper away from Gare de Lyon and within a leisurely stroll from both Opéra Bastille and the Marais, you'll find the quaint Bistrot de la Gare. This bistro, steeped in the rich traditions of Paris, invites you to partake in an exquisite gastronomic adventure.

Bistrot de la Gare presents a cozy and welcoming setting, ideal for a relaxed midday meal, a dinner before the theater, or a romantic night out. The ambiance, characterized by exposed brickwork, classic wooden fixtures, and gentle illumination, offers a snug and inviting space, while the scent of freshly crafted cuisine stimulates the senses. The culinary offerings at Bistrot de la Gare pay homage to the finest of French gastronomy.

The chef takes pride in using fresh, in-season produce to create mouthwatering meals that are as aesthetical

Begin your dining experience with traditional French starters such as oeufs durs mayonnaise or rillettes de canard, accompanied by freshly baked bread. For your entrée, choose from beloved dishes like coq au vin, steak frites, or blanquette de veau. Make sure to save space for dessert, allowing yourself the pleasure of French classics such as crème brûlée or tarte tatin. Bistrot de la Gare is proud of its carefully selected wine list, featuring an array of French wines that perfectly complement your meal. The considerate and professional staff will ensure your dining experience is seamless, offering recommendations and attending to your dining needs. Whether you're a frequent visitor to Paris or discovering its charms for the first time, Bistrot de la Gare is a must-visit for anyone seeking a genuine taste of Parisian culinary heritage. The combination of its inviting atmosphere, delectable food, and hospitable service makes for an unforgettable encounter.

Please Note:

It is advised to book your table in advance, particularly during busy times and weekends. The dress code is smart casual.

La Chope des Puces

Address: 122 Rue des Rosiers, 93400 Saint-Ouen-sur-Seine, France
Positioned in the vivacious Saint-Ouen Flea Market, surrounded by a maze of alleyways filled with unique treasures, sits La Chope des Puces. Not far from the Porte de Clignancourt metro, this genuine Parisian brasserie offers a refreshing retreat from the hustle and bustle and a chance to dive into the lively flea market life.

La Chope des Puces radiates a relaxed yet animated vibe, drawing in both avid flea market goers and locals in search of a momentary respite. The interior, with its raw brick walls, retro posters, and inviting lighting, sets a hospitable scene, while the background hum of conversation and clinking glasses adds to the dynamic atmosphere. The brasserie's menu spotlights classic French comfort fare, made with fresh, seasonal produce. Whether you're after a quick snack or a more substantial meal, the bistro caters to a variety of tastes. Kick off your culinary exploration with time-honored French starters such as escargots à la Bourguignonne or soupe à l'oignon gratinée, perfect for the cooler days. As a main, dive into satisfying plates like steak tartare, confit de canard, or boudin noir aux pommes, each served with traditional French sides. Be sure to sample the assortment of regional cheeses or treat yourself to a house-made tarte tatin to conclude your meal on a sweet note. La Chope des Puces offers a selection of French wines, beers, and spirits to enhance your dining experience. The warm and informed staff will add to your enjoyment, providing suggestions and ensuring a pleasant visit. Whether your flea market adventure was fruitful or not, La Chope des Puces provides an ideal haven to relax and recharge. With its authentic ambiance, scrumptious food, and welcoming service, it embodies the true spirit of Parisian flea market culture.

Please Note:

Cash is often the preferred method of payment, though cards may be accepted. The dress code is casual.

Le Garde-Manger

Address: 8 Rue Meissonier, 75017 Paris, France

Discover Parisian Delicacies at Le Garde-Manger. In the upscale 17th arrondissement of Paris, amidst grand thoroughfares and stately Haussmannian architecture, you'll discover Le Garde-Manger, which translates to "the pantry." This endearing eatery, with its striking burgundy terrazzo exterior and exquisite painted ceilings, promises an authentic Parisian dining experience in a cordial and welcoming setting.

Le Garde-Manger has a rich heritage, having evolved from a neighborhood delicatessen to a cherished dining spot while preserving its original charm. The gleaming meat slicer and the terrazzo frontage are nostalgic elements of its history, and the inviting interior offers a warm and cozy dining atmosphere. The menu at Le Garde-Manger is a testament to seasonal, superior ingredients, highlighting the produce of local farms and artisans. Chef Etienne, the culinary maestro, is devoted to crafting simple yet sumptuous dishes, blending traditional methods with contemporary flair.

Enjoy the daily specials presented in the display case, featuring rotating seasonal specialties. For something lighter, opt for homemade salads or sandwiches made with fresh bread and choice ingredients. If you're in the mood for something more substantial, select from classic French dishes like coq au vin or blanquette de veau, each prepared with meticulous care. Don't overlook the enticing array of desserts, including house-baked pastries such as éclairs and mille-feuilles.

Please Note:

- Smart casual attire is suggested, and it's wise to reserve a table in advance, particularly during peak dining hours.

Le Garde-Manger extends an invitation to both locals and travelers alike to immerse themselves in an authentic Parisian gastronomic adventure. This delightful haven pairs its inviting atmosphere with delectable fare and gracious service, providing a tranquil haven to unwind and embrace the quintessential Parisian lifestyle.

Proximity: Roland-Garros (Tennis & Boxing)

Le Petit Rôtisseur
Address: 23 Rue du 8 Mai 1945, 33500 Les Billaux, France

Immerse yourself in the enticing scent of roasting fowl as you enter Le Petit Rôtisseur, a Parisian sanctuary devoted to the culinary craft of rotisserie. Nestled in the bustling [insert neighborhood name] area, this quaint eatery presents an enchanting journey for both residents and tourists in search of authentic French gastronomy. Dubbed "The Little Roaster," Le Petit Rôtisseur prides itself on its singular focus: expertly crafted rotisserie chicken. Their flagship offering, a whole chicken expertly seasoned and slow-roasted, emerges with a crisp, amber exterior and succulent, flavorful flesh. This mouthwatering showpiece takes center stage, accompanied by a variety of tempting side dishes. Though rotisserie chicken is the cornerstone, Le Petit Rôtisseur caters to a range of tastes.

Expand your protein palette and enjoy the rich taste of rotisserie duck, the robust flavors of rotisserie pork, or opt for rotisserie vegetables as a plant-based alternative. Select from traditional French accompaniments such as roasted potatoes, fresh seasonal produce, or a crisp green salad. Conclude with a confection, Treat yourself to a house-made dessert, with options like velvety chocolate mousse or a vibrant fruit tart.

Le Petit Rôtisseur exudes a convivial and welcoming environment, ideal for a leisurely lunch or an unhurried evening meal. The interior, with its bare brick walls, homey wooden fixtures, and viewable kitchen, offers a snug and genial setting where patrons can observe the chickens as they roast to perfection. Le Petit Rôtisseur is more than just a place to dine; it's an authentic Parisian experience. The congenial and diligent staff greets each guest warmly, ensuring a seamless meal from start to finish. Amidst the fragrant aroma of roasting poultry and the gentle hum of conversation, a sense of camaraderie and connection permeates the air.

Remember:
- Reservations are recommended, especially during peak hours and on weekends.
- Dress code is casual.

La Gauloise Brasserie
59 Av. de la Motte-Picquet, 75015 Paris, France

Tucked away in the bustling 15th district of Paris, La Gauloise Brasserie extends an invitation to embark on a gastronomic voyage through time. This esteemed French establishment, with over a hundred years of history, provides a cozy setting for patrons to enjoy quintessential French cuisine amidst Parisians.

La Gauloise, a name that harks back to the ancient denizens of Gaul, is steeped in a storied past. It has stood the test of time, becoming an endearing local fixture and serving countless Parisians across multiple generations. The walls, adorned with vintage photographs and classic décor, transport patrons to a former epoch in the city's rich tapestry of life.

The brasserie's menu is a tribute to time-honored French gastronomic practices, with a selection of robust and soulful dishes made from the freshest ingredients each season brings. The chef pays homage to these culinary customs while infusing a touch of creativity, offering a repertoire that is both reassuringly familiar and refreshingly engaging. Begin your dining experience with traditional French starters such as escargots à la Bourguignonne (snails bathed in garlic butter) or soupe à l'oignon gratinée (golden-browned French onion soup), ideal for the cooler Parisian days. Continue with revered French entrées like coq au vin (chicken stewed in red wine), steak-frites (grilled steak accompanied by fries), or boudin noir aux pommes (blood sausage served with apples). Each dish is crafted with precision and a keen eye for detail. Ensure your meal concludes on a high note with an array of regional French cheeses or a homemade tarte tatin (caramelized apple tart), a sweet finale to your dining experience.

La Gauloise Brasserie is a haven for those longing to immerse themselves in genuine Parisian dining, whether they are city dwellers or travelers in search of true local flavors. Between its inviting charm, classic culinary offerings, and amiable service, the brasserie stands as a testament to the enduring allure of Parisian culture.

Remember:
- Reservations are recommended, especially during peak hours and on weekends.
- Dress code is casual and smart.

Proximity: Champ de Mars Arena (Judo & Wrestling)

Le Soufflé

Address: 36 Rue du Mont Thabor, 75001 Paris, France

Tucked away in Paris's vibrant 1st arrondissement, Le Soufflé stands as a culinary sanctuary dedicated to perfecting both savory and sweet soufflés. Since its inception in 1961, this quaint eatery has been celebrated for its gastronomic finesse and inviting atmosphere, drawing both residents and tourists. Le Soufflé is a testament to family tradition, with its operation spanning multiple generations. Guests are embraced by an atmosphere of warmth and nostalgia, accentuated by the classic décor, complete with rustic brickwork and antique allure. True to its name, Le Soufflé's menu is a tribute to this airy delicacy. Patrons can choose from an extensive array of soufflés, satisfying a broad spectrum of tastes. Savor the savory with choices like the timeless soufflé au fromage or explore unique tastes such as the soufflé à la langoustine or soufflé aux cèpes. For a more delicate choice, the soufflé aux légumes offers a medley of fresh, seasonal produce. The sweet finale is equally impressive, with offerings like the indulgent soufflé au chocolat or the seasonal soufflé aux fruits. While soufflés are the highlight, Le Soufflé also presents a range of classic French dishes. Begin with traditional starters such as escargots à la Bourguignonne or the iconic soupe à l'oignon gratinée. Main dishes include the quintessential steak frites and the rich coq au vin.

Le Soufflé is not just about the exquisite fare; it's about the authentic Parisian experience it provides. The staff's enthusiasm for their craft shines through as they assist guests with menu selections and recommendations, all while ensuring a seamless dining encounter. The vibrant buzz of conversation and the melody of glassware contribute to a welcoming community vibe.

For both connoisseurs of soufflés and those seeking a genuine slice of Parisian gastronomy, Le Soufflé promises an enchanting culinary journey. This establishment is a celebration of soufflé artistry, set within a cozy ambiance and supported by gracious hospitality, making it a cornerstone of Parisian gastronomic delight.

Remember:
- Reservations are recommended, especially during peak hours.
- Dress code is casual

Le Café du Trocadéro

Address: 8 Place du Trocadéro et du 11 Novembre, 75116 Paris, France

Envision the gentle warmth of the sun in Paris as you enjoy a cup of coffee, with the magnificent Eiffel Tower unfolding before your eyes. This picturesque scene is part of the daily charm at Le Café du Trocadéro, an enchanting venue that presents awe-inspiring vistas and traditional French fare in the core of the 16th arrondissement.

Le Café du Trocadéro epitomizes the essence of Paris. Located in the esteemed Place du Trocadéro et du 11 Novembre, it has evolved over the years, culminating in a 2017 refurbishment that maintained its art deco allure while infusing contemporary enhancements. The restaurant's interior is bathed in sunlight, thanks to its large glass facades and thoughtfully positioned mirrors, fostering a luminous and welcoming space.

Le Café du Trocadéro's menu pays homage to classic French gastronomy with an emphasis on seasonal produce. Whether you're in the mood for an unhurried breakfast, a laid-back lunch, or a tranquil dinner, the offerings are sure to delight your palate.

Begin your day with quintessential Parisian breakfast selections, including freshly baked pastries and croissants, paired with your choice of coffee or tea. For your midday or evening meal, explore a variety of time-honored French fare such as:

Salads: Ideal for those preferring a lighter fare, featuring fresh ingredients in inventive blends.

Sandwiches: Prepared with freshly baked bread and flavorful fillings, perfect for a swift, satisfying meal.

Entrees: Savor the essence of French culinary tradition with options like steak frites (grilled steak with French fries) or coq au vin (chicken cooked in red wine).

Be sure to peruse the enticing dessert menu, showcasing traditional French confections and other delectable sweets.

The true magic of Le Café du Trocadéro extends beyond its cuisine, rooted in its exceptional setting and mesmerizing atmosphere. Revel in the Parisian sun and take in the stunning panorama of the Eiffel Tower, an experience that's truly etched in memory. The vibrant setting, buzzing with conversations of both locals and visitors, fosters a sense of community and connection. The establishment's hospitable and attentive team is committed to ensuring a cordial and inviting dining experience.

For both local denizens and tourists in pursuit of an authentic Parisian encounter, Le Café du Trocadéro is the ideal haven. With its extraordinary views, exquisite dishes, and congenial atmosphere, it stands as a sanctuary where one can unwind, indulge, and embrace the soul of Paris.

Remember:
- Reservations are recommended, especially during peak hours and on weekends.
- Dress code is casual

Bao Family - Trendy Asian fusion fare

Address: 116 Rue St Denis, 75002 Paris, France

Seeking an epicurean escapade? Venture to Bao Family, the chic eatery in Paris that promises a gastronomic odyssey through the dynamic tastes of Asian fusion fare. Esteemed by both natives and tourists for its original and whimsical culinary creations, this establishment stands as a beacon for those in pursuit of an extraordinary meal.

At Bao Family, Asian cuisine undergoes a transformation. The menu artfully merges classic elements and methodologies from diverse Asian traditions, crafting dishes that are at once recognizable and thrillingly novel. Commence your gastronomic quest with a variety of small, shareable plates. Envision golden gyoza stuffed with unconventional fillings such as duck confit, or fiery, Korean-inspired tacos cradling tender bulgogi beef.

As you progress to the entrées, immerse yourself in a tapestry of tastes with choices such as: Smoky Vietnamese pho, its deep broth enveloping supple noodles. Intense Thai curries, exploding with aromatic spices and verdant veggies. Japanese-influenced noodle plates, from savory ramens to cool, zesty soba. The bao buns, from which the restaurant derives its name, are not to be overlooked. These pillowy parcels arrive brimming with a variety of luscious fillings, ranging from the traditional char siu pork to creative vegetarian options. Bao Family's spirited essence is reflected not only in its cuisine but also in its setting. The décor is a fusion of Asian motifs and contemporary chic, crafting an atmosphere that's both fashionable and welcoming. An open kitchen offers a glimpse into the chefs' realm, where gastronomic alchemy takes place. The ambiance is further amplified by a soundtrack infused with Asian melodies, contributing to the vivacious vibe.

Remember:
- Reservations are recommended, especially during peak hours and on weekends.
- Dress code is casual.

Île-de-France options:

Proximity: Stade Jean-Bouin (Rugby Sevens)

Café Trama

Address: 83 rue du Cherche-Midi, 75006 Paris, France

Nestled in the heart of Paris' vibrant 6th arrondissement, Café Trama beckons with the aroma of roasting poultry and the promise of a delightful culinary experience. This contemporary café is a local favorite, offering a delectable menu featuring revisited classics and a warm and inviting atmosphere. Café Trama transcends ordinary café offerings by infusing classic French cuisine with inventive flair, utilizing premium components and innovative culinary methods. Delight your palate with appetizers such as the lamb sweetbreads paired with fig terrine, or the sautéed girolle mushrooms crowned with a poached egg. When it comes to the main dishes, allow yourself to be enticed by their reimagined croque-monsieur, accentuated with truffle-scented salt and matured Comté cheese. Additional entrées feature succulent duck breast and rotating selections of fresh fish. For both Paris dwellers and visitors desiring an authentic taste of the city's culinary heritage, Café Trama promises an enchanting encounter. It stands out as a culinary haven where one can indulge in exquisite fare, experience heartfelt hospitality, and capture the essence of Parisian neighborhood life.

Remember:
- Reservations are recommended, especially during peak hours.
- Dress code is casual.

Proximity: Stade Vélodrome (Marseille)

Le Petit Nice

Address: 14 Rue Corniche Kennedy, 13007 Marseille, France

The esteemed Le Petit Nice Passedat, a culinary gem with three Michelin stars, graces the city of Marseille, France. Perched along the Anse de Maldormé, diners are treated to spectacular vistas of the sea and a dining experience that lingers in memory. Under the guidance of Chef Gérald Passedat, this family-operated venue has stood as a pillar of culinary excellence for nearly a century, continually reinventing the essence of Mediterranean flavors.

Step into an ambiance of sophistication, where the grandeur of the Mediterranean unfolds through expansive windows, framing the sea and the cityscape of Marseille. The décor, both minimalist and contemporary, ensures that the focus remains on the visual feast outside and the gastronomic delights presented.

Le Petit Nice celebrates the freshest, seasonal produce, with a special emphasis on treasures from the Mediterranean. Chef Passedat's inventive culinary artistry elevates these offerings into dishes that are both visually stunning and rich in taste, often exploring an array of textures and palates. The menu is dynamic, offering a taste of what might be encountered. Begin with dishes such as carpaccio of sea urchin or ravioli stuffed with langoustine. Main courses may include sea bass enveloped in a salt crust or monkfish accompanied by a bouillabaisse reduction. Plant-based selections are also crafted, reflecting the fertile lands that border the sea.

A Gastronomic Journey:

For enthusiasts of fine dining and travelers with a discerning palate, Le Petit Nice stands as a must-visit destination. It promises an unparalleled fusion of innovative dishes, exceptional service, and a setting that captures the heart of French culinary tradition.

Remember:
As a three-Michelin-starred restaurant, Le Petit Nice caters to a specific clientele and requires reservations well in advance. Dress code is smart casual.

Be prepared for a high-end dining experience with a corresponding price range.

Chez Michel

Address: 10 Rue de Belzunce, 75010 Paris, France

Tucked away in the bustling 10th district of Paris, Chez Michel stands as a gem for those yearning for a taste of authentic French fare with a contemporary flair. Thierry Breton, the original visionary behind this cozy bistro, has handed the reins to chef Masahiro

Kawai. Kawai skillfully infuses new life into time-honored recipes while keeping the eatery's inviting essence intact. Step into Chez Michel and find yourself enveloped by the quintessential Parisian charm. Picture the warm glow of rustic wooden furnishings, quirky trinkets lining the walls, and the welcoming embrace of exposed wooden beams. It's a unique spot that radiates the heart and soul of Paris. The menu at Chez Michel is a voyage through the annals of French gastronomy, with a twist of modernity. Kick off your feast with satisfying starters like the rich sobrasada paired with creamy mashed potatoes, topped with a fried egg and sweet quince paste, or dive into the Gnocchi with a robust wild-boar bolognese.

Entrees to Captivate the Senses: Feast on beloved creations such as the Kig Ha Farz (a classic Breton buckwheat pancake), or choose from options like succulent duck breast, the catch of the day, or a plant-based dish. Wrap up your meal with a sweet note, perhaps with the iconic Paris-Brest, its choux pastry hugging a luscious praline cream, or a comforting slice of pumpkin cake.

The bistro's warm and efficient service makes every visit a pleasure. Soak in the genuine Parisian vibe and rub elbows with the locals who cherish this spot. The restaurant's modern zest is beautifully balanced with its rich history, reminding patrons of its roots in this lively quarter. Chez Michel is a destination worth discovering. It's a place where the passion for fresh ingredients, reinvented classics, and heartfelt service come together to capture the essence of the Parisian community spirit.

Le Pressoir d'Argent

Address: Pl. de la Comédie, 33000 Bordeaux, France

Le Pressoir d'Argent, perched on the first floor of the InterContinental Bordeaux Le Grand Hotel in the heart of Bordeaux, France, is a gem of a restaurant with a Michelin star to its name. It promises an upscale and polished dining adventure. Under the helm of the famed chef Gordon Ramsay, the restaurant prides itself on a menu that's both elegant and inventive, highlighting fresh, local produce and a wine collection that spans a staggering 1,500 varieties.

As you enter Le Pressoir d'Argent, you're immediately wrapped in an aura of luxury and refinement. Picture yourself dining under the glow of sophisticated chandeliers, surrounded by sumptuous fabrics, all while taking in the breathtaking vistas of the city. It's the perfect backdrop for a memorable celebration.

Chef Ramsay's culinary prowess shines through in a menu that marries time-honored French cooking with a dash of contemporary flair. Le Pressoir d'Argent is an experience that transcends the culinary. Enjoy the highest level of service from a team that's as knowledgeable as they are considerate, ensuring every aspect of your meal is flawless. Dive into an award-winning wine list, expertly selected to pair beautifully with your meal. This is the place to immerse yourself in an atmosphere of grandeur and indulgence, whether you're marking a special event or looking for an enchanting evening out. For both locals and travelers in search of an exceptional dining affair, Le Pressoir d'Argent stands out as a celebration of culinary artistry. With its standout dishes, top-notch service, and a wine list that's second to none, it invites you to relish in top-tier ingredients and the joy of upscale dining.

Remember:
- Reservations are highly recommended, as Le Pressoir d'Argent is a popular restaurant.
- Dress code is smart casual.
- Be prepared for a high-end dining experience with a corresponding price range.

La Tupina

Address: 6 rue Porte-de-la-Monnaie, 33000 Bordeaux, France

Established back in '68, La Tupina is a gem in Bordeaux, France, famed for its homage to classic South West French fare. Nestled in the old quarter on rue Porte de la Monnaie, this family-operated spot has won the hearts of locals and is a go-to for anyone craving genuine tastes in a cozy setting. Wander into La Tupina and find yourself in an enchanting, welcoming space. Picture the rustic elegance of bare brick walls, soft lighting, and comfy seats. The interior, with its French country house vibe, adds a real, down-home feel. La Tupina is all about fresh, in-season produce from nearby farms. Their offerings celebrate the South West's rich food heritage, with menu items like. Kick things off with timeless favorites such as a hearty country pork pâté or snails swimming in garlicky Bordelaise butter. Dig into their famous lamb shoulder confit with fresh beans, or a juicy duck breast draped in cherry sauce. There are tasty vegetarian picks too, featuring garden-fresh veggies cooked in time-honored styles. Wrap up your dining adventure with a local sweet like the canelé, a petite custard cake with a crunchy caramel shell, or the classic tarte Tatin, a caramelized apple delight served upside down.

The warm, caring team works hard to make your meal a standout, always ready to go above and beyond to ensure you're feeling right at home. Dive into the real Bordeaux vibe, cherished by those who live there and perfectly capturing the city's essence. Take in the deep-rooted food traditions of South West France with dishes made with love and a deft touch. For locals or visitors chasing the true Bordeaux flavor, La Tupina is a joyous spot. Its inviting ambiance, scrumptious cuisine, and top-notch service make it an ideal place to indulge in the South West's palate and embrace the spirit of Bordeaux.

Remember:

- Reservations are recommended, especially during peak hours.

L'Argentin Grill

Address: 2 Rue du Rouet, 13006 Marseille, France

Discover L'Argentin, a top-notch steakhouse and wine bar nestled in the vibrant heart of Paris, France. This place is a haven for those who appreciate the finer things in life, offering a ritzy vibe, top-tier cuts of beef, and a wine selection that's second to none. It's the go-to spot for meat lovers and wine aficionados looking for a touch of class in their dining experience.

Picture yourself walking into a world of sophistication. L'Argentin welcomes you with luxurious seating, inviting warm lights, and chic decor that together craft a cozy yet classy space. Whether you're marking a milestone, impressing clients at lunch, or planning a night of romance, the setting here is just right.

At the heart of L'Argentin's menu is a tribute to Argentinean fare, especially its world-class steaks. The restaurant prides itself on offering beef from grass-fed Argentine cattle, celebrated for its distinctive taste and buttery tenderness.

Kick off your feast with mouth-watering starters like flavorful empanadas or spicy chorizo sausage. Take your pick from an array of steak cuts including the juicy ribeye, classic New York strip, or the succulent tenderloin, all grilled to your liking and bursting with rich, meaty goodness. Elevate your steak with side dishes that range from crispy French fries and creamy spinach to a medley of roasted veggies. Dive into a wine list that spans from Argentina's finest to South America's hidden gems. Let the friendly staff guide you to the ideal wine pairing for your dish.

L'Argentin is an experience that goes beyond the plate. Enjoy top-notch service from a team that's all about making your visit smooth and memorable. Soak in the posh and polished atmosphere, tailor-made for creating unforgettable moments. Delight in the culinary heritage of Argentina, with its standout flavors and premium ingredients.

Remember:
- As a high-end restaurant, reservations are recommended, especially during peak hours.
- Dress code is likely smart casual, but checking their website or contacting the restaurant directly is recommended for confirmation.

Budget friendly options

Here are some budget-friendly dining options near the Olympic venues for those looking to experience great food without breaking the bank:

Paris:

Proximity: Stade de France

Stoño - Lively street food court with international options

For those attending the Olympics and seeking an energetic and varied place to eat close to the Stade de France, Stoño is a fantastic choice. Here's a closer look at what this bustling street food hub brings to the table. Stoño buzzes with the lively charm of Parisian streets, nestled just a stone's throw from the Stade de France. As the Olympic Games unfold, this spot is sure to be alive with excitement. Visitors can immerse themselves in the dynamic vibe, rub shoulders with sports fans from all over the world, and dive into a smorgasbord of global dishes.

The standout feature of Stoño is its eclectic mix of international eats. Whether you're craving the comfort of French crêpes, the zest of Vietnamese banh mi, or the spice of Thai curries, you'll find it all here. It's a place where your taste buds can go on an adventure, discovering a world of flavors without stepping outside the food court's energetic atmosphere.

Vegetarian and vegan dishes

Stoño also serves up a variety of vegetarian and vegan delights, ensuring that everyone has something to savor. You can wrap your hands around a hearty falafel wrap, dig into a nutrient-rich Buddha bowl, or sample a selection of international dishes that are free from animal products. As a street food destination, Stoño is all about delivering delicious food that won't cost you a fortune, making it a smart pick for Olympic goers watching their wallets. The stalls and trucks dish out tasty meals and treats at prices that are easy on the pocket, so you can feast on diverse cuisines without fretting over the cost.

Located conveniently near the Stade de France, Stoño is the perfect place to grab a bite before or after catching an Olympic event. It's just a quick walk away, so you can refuel with ease and get back to the excitement. More than just food, Stoño offers a festive atmosphere that echoes the Olympic energy. With shared seating, potential live entertainment, and a crowd that's both sporty and food-loving, this street food court is an experience in itself.

Crous de Paris

Crous de Paris is a network of university eateries offering affordable meals, ideal for Olympic visitors on a budget. Near venues like the Stade de France, these cafeterias could be a practical option for a quick, wallet-friendly meal. As student cafeterias, Crous de Paris is all about providing meals at prices that are student-friendly. You can expect to get a complete meal with a main, side, and drink for approximately €3-5. On the menu, you'll find straightforward yet hearty French staples like steak frites, quiche, and pasta, focusing on satisfying and nourishing food rather than gourmet offerings.

The setup is traditional cafeteria-style, with various stations offering hot mains, sides, desserts, and drinks. You'll pick and choose your items as you move down the line. While the prices are great, the variety can be limited, especially for those with specific dietary needs like vegan or vegetarian. The menu tends to stick to simple French classics without a wide international range. Expect a straightforward dining environment. The Crous cafeterias are designed with a functional, no-frills approach, featuring basic tables and minimal decor, catering to students in need of a quick meal.

With numerous locations throughout Paris, including several near major Olympic venues like the Stade de France, these cafeterias are conveniently located for a quick stop. For Olympic visitors prioritizing savings over ambiance, Crous de Paris offers a solid alternative for an affordable, filling meal close to the action. Simple and satisfying, the basic French cafe fare will keep you fueled for the events ahead.

Proximity: Golf National

La Grange aux Loups

Nestled near the Golf National course, soon to be the 2024 Paris Olympics' golfing hotspot, you'll find La Grange aux Loups, a charming country inn that promises a laid-back dining experience. Location:14 Route de Bailly, 78470 Saint-Rémy-lès-Chevreuse, France. Online at: www.lagrangeauxloups.com

A stone's throw from the esteemed Golf National in the quaint village of Saint-Rémy-lès-Chevreuse, this inn sits in a lovingly restored 17th-century farmhouse. Amidst gardens and pastoral views, its dining rooms and terrace exude a homey, unpretentious vibe. Expect a menu brimming with traditional French country dishes, crafted from locally-sourced, seasonal ingredients, and even from the inn's own garden. Think robust stews, sizzling grilled meats, fresh garden veggies, and indulgent sweets. Celebrated for its "farmhouse inn" approach, La Grange aux Loups brings the freshest farm produce straight to your plate. Hours of operation are from Wed-Sun: 12pm-2:30pm / 7pm-9:30pm while they are closed Mon and Tue.

Minutes from the Olympic golf action, this inn is a serene retreat, serving up genuine, top-notch French cuisine. Booking ahead is smart, especially when the Olympics roll around.

Le Bon Bec - Neighborhood Bistro Charm

Close to Saint-Germain-en-Laye, and not far from the Golf National, Le Bon Bec is a cozy bistro that's a hit with locals and visitors alike. Location: 15 Rue Leroy, 78100 Saint-Germain-en-Laye, France

In the bustling heart of Saint-Germain-en-Laye, a mere 10-minute drive from the golfing excitement, this bistro offers a warm welcome with its bare stone walls, wooden beams, and quintessential French flair. Whether you're seated inside or out on the terrace, the atmosphere is friendly and laid-back. The menu is a homage to classic bistro cuisine, featuring quality ingredients from the region. Signature dishes include the likes of French onion soup, steak frites, coq au vin, and a selection of seafood. They also serve a great-value set lunch menu. Hours: Tue-Sat, Lunch: 12 pm - 2:30 pm and dinner: 7pm - 10pm.

Le Bon Bec is a fantastic choice for Olympic goers, offering affordability and convenience near the golf venue. Its genuine bistro setting is the perfect place to unwind with hearty French classics after a day of sports spectating. Remember to reserve your spot, especially during the Olympics, to savor a slice of French culinary tradition in this charming neighborhood spot.

Tahiti (Teahupo'o):

Roulotte de Mariella - A Local Favorite for Polynesian Eats

Roulotte de Mariella is a much-loved food truck dishing out tasty and budget-friendly Polynesian cuisine on the island of Tahiti, just a hop from the Teahupo'o surf spot, an Olympic venue. Located at PK 38 Côté Mer, Teahupo'o, Tahiti. This food truck has won hearts with its genuine Tahitian dishes, made from the freshest local ingredients. On the menu: meals like Poisson Cru, Tahiti's iconic raw fish salad, Slow-cooked, savory Porc à la Roulotte, Hearty chicken or veggie curries with a coconut twist, Grilled catch of the day, Po'e, a traditional banana treat. Simple yet vibrant island flavors define their food, available as plate lunches or by portion, emphasizing top-notch local seafood and produce. Working Hours are from Mon-Sat: 10am - 3pm while they are closed on Sun. For a true taste of island life and a budget-friendly meal, Roulotte de Mariella is the go-to spot for surfing fans at Teahupo'o.

Le Bounty - A Gathering of Affordable Food Trucks

Le Bounty is a lively ensemble of food trucks, offering an array of inexpensive dining choices near the Teahupo'o surf break, an Olympic venue. Location: Teahupo'o village, along the coastal road, southwest coast of Tahiti. Le Bounty features a vibrant lineup of food trucks and stands, complete with picnic tables and awnings for outdoor dining. The food includes Polynesian plates with poisson cru, curries, and grilled fish, Rotisserie chicken, Tahitian chow mein, Crepe stands, Pizza trucks, Asian noodle bowls, Fresh tropical juices and smoothies.

The atmosphere is casual and perfect for a quick meal between surfing events. Working hours are Mostly open from late morning to early evening, with dishes generally under $15. Le Bounty is a fun, wallet-friendly way to enjoy local Polynesian flavors and international street food while soaking in the Tahitian vistas.

Le Caillou - Beachside Snack Bar Delights

Le Caillou is a casual beachside snack bar in Teahupo'o village, Tahiti, offering convenient and affordable eats close to the iconic surf break, soon to be an Olympic venue. Location: Central Teahupo'o, along the coastal road. This simple spot is known for its walk-up service and outdoor seating just off the beach. The menu includes: Grilled fish platters with local catches, Po'e, a traditional banana dessert, Tahitian fried chicken, Coconut bread, Firi Firi (beef skewers), Fresh fruit salads and juices, Cooked on an open grill, the food has a smoky flavor, with generous portions at great prices, mostly under $10. Hours: 10am - 6pm daily.

Le Caillou is the ideal place for Olympic spectators to enjoy affordable, authentic Tahitian cuisine in a laid-back beach setting. With these casual and diverse dining options, Olympic visitors can indulge in the local food scene without breaking the bank.

Transportation costs and planning specific to Paris

Experiencing the Paris 2024 Olympic Games is set to be a momentous occasion, with efficient city navigation playing a pivotal role during this exhilarating time. This section explores the specialized transportation strategies devised to manage the surge of participants, ensuring seamless and accessible transit throughout your Olympic escapade.

A Pledge to Public Transport:

The Paris 2024 Olympic Games' organizing committee is dedicated to delivering dependable and effective transit solutions for all visitors, with a focus on sustainability and inclusivity. Their strategy involves:

Upgraded Public Transport Network:

- Boosted Frequency: The public transportation system, including buses, metros, and trains, will operate at a 15% higher frequency than the usual summer schedules, reducing wait times and increasing the availability of transport options.

- Network Expansion: The expansion of Paris Metro Line 14, set to complete in June 2024, will provide a direct route from Orly Airport to Saint-Denis Pleyel, improving overall network connectivity.

Specialized Services for Accredited Individuals:

- Exclusive Fleet: A specific fleet of vehicles, including buses and minibusses, will be reserved for athletes, delegation members, and media personnel, facilitating prompt transfers between accommodations and event locations.

Emphasizing Sustainability:

The Paris 2024 Games are set to lead by example in sustainability, incorporating hydrogen-powered vehicles on a large scale for the first time in Olympic history. This progressive move underlines the potential of clean energy and sets the stage for a more eco-friendly future.

Universal Accessibility:

The Games' organizers are devoted to creating an inclusive environment where all spectators can partake in the festivities, regardless of mobility challenges. This is achieved through:

- Assured Travel Times: A network of 185 kilometers of roads will be designated, when necessary, to ensure that every event is no more than 30 minutes away from the Olympic Village, facilitating quick and hassle-free travel for all.
- Emphasis on Public Transport: Public transportation is inherently more accommodating for individuals with disabilities, often featuring specialized facilities and services.

Cycling: A Lasting Eco-Friendly Legacy:

The Paris 2024 Games are also endorsing cycling as a sustainable and health-conscious travel option. The existing cycling infrastructure will be extended to encompass 415 kilometers across the Paris region, with an additional 20,000 bike parking spots. This initiative not only promotes an eco-friendly mode of travel for visitors but also serves as a long-term benefit for the city's residents.

Strategizing Your Transit: While the organizers have a detailed plan in place, personal transport planning remains crucial. Here are some recommendations:

- App-Based Navigation: Get acquainted with navigation apps such as Google Maps or Citymapper to chart your routes and pinpoint the most effective public transport choices.
- Paris Visite Pass: Consider acquiring a Paris Visite Pass, which grants unlimited access to public transit within selected zones for a set duration.
- Cycling Exploration: If it suits you, think about bike rentals to experience the city and make use of the expanded cycling routes.
- Anticipate Delays: Despite the goal of seamless operations, unforeseen delays may still occur. Stay adaptable and patient during your travels.

By grasping the transportation arrangements and leveraging the provided tools, you can ensure a fluid and delightful experience while traversing Paris for the 2024 Olympic Games. Embracing sustainable travel methods like cycling will not only enhance the success of the Games but also leave a positive ecological imprint.

Revealing Transportation Costs: Budgeting for Paris 2024 Travel

While the Paris 2024 Olympic Games emphasize public transit, being aware of the associated costs and considering other travel alternatives will facilitate efficient city navigation.

Public Transportation:

Fare System: Paris employs a fare system for its public transport network, with tickets available at metro stations or via mobile apps.

Fare Options:

- Single Journey Tickets: These tickets allow for one trip on any mode of public transportation within a specific time frame. Anticipated prices are from €1.90 for a central Paris trip to slightly more for suburban travel.
- Travel Cards: A Paris Visite Pass for unlimited travel in certain zones over a chosen duration (1 to 5 days) may be ideal. Costs vary based on zone reach and duration. A 1-day pass for zones 1-3 is estimated at around €22.80.
- Navigo Easy Pass (for longer visits): For extended stays, the Navigo Easy Pass, a top-up card offering unlimited zone-specific travel, is a practical option. A nominal fee for the card itself is required, with additional charges for travel credits.

Bus Hubs:

Key bus terminals in Paris include:

- Gare Routière Internationale de Paris at Porte de Bagnolet: Serving long-distance domestic and European routes. Increased activity and potential delays are likely during the Olympics.
- Smaller bus stations: These cater to regional and suburban lines. Verify routes and timetables in advance.

Car Parking:

Given the anticipated rise in traffic and possible road closures near Olympic sites, driving in Paris may not be advisable. However, if driving is necessary:

- Scarce On-Street Parking: Street parking in central Paris is limited and typically costly, with expected rate hikes during the Olympics.
- Public Parking Facilities: These offer a more regulated parking environment but can be pricey. Pre-booking near your lodging or intended locations is advised, particularly for long-term parking.
- Park-and-Ride Options: Consider using park-and-ride facilities outside central Paris, enabling you to park your vehicle and take public transport to your final destination.

Alternative Travel Modes:

- Cycling: With the focus on cycling, renting a bike to independently explore the city is a viable option, especially given the expanded cycling network.
- Ride-Hailing Services: Ride-sharing apps like Uber and Lyft provide convenient travel for shorter distances, though higher pricing may apply during peak times or high-demand periods.
- Taxis: Taxis are widely available but can be more expensive than public transport. They're suitable for late-night trips or when public transit isn't an option.

Efficient Travel Planning:

- Do Your Homework: Familiarize yourself with the public transit routes from your accommodation to Olympic venues and other places of interest.
- Advance Ticket Purchases: To avoid lines at ticket kiosks, especially during busy times, buy your tickets or passes ahead of time.

- Install Mobile Apps: Apps like Google Maps or Citymapper will assist in planning routes and finding the most efficient public transit options.
- Stay Adaptable: Be ready to modify your travel itinerary and remain patient, as delays can happen despite efforts for a smooth operation.

By comprehending the transportation choices, pricing, and planning your trips wisely, you can effortlessly navigate Paris during the 2024 Olympic Games and create an unforgettable experience.

Additional expenses to consider

When orchestrating a visit to the Paris 2024 Olympic Games, it's crucial to account for various expenses beyond just travel, lodging, and event tickets. Here are key considerations to manage your finances effectively:
- Culinary Expenses: Anticipate the cost of enjoying French gastronomy while attending the Games. Allocate funds for daily meals, including breakfast, lunch, and dinner. To economize, seek out more affordable eateries or purchase groceries for some meals.
- Leisure and Sightseeing: Plan to allocate resources for experiencing Parisian and other local attractions, museums, or historical sites. Set aside funds for entrance fees and guided excursions to enrich your visit. Look for cost-saving opportunities such as discounts or complimentary attractions.
- Memorabilia and Merchandise: Allocate a portion of your budget for keepsakes or official Olympic merchandise to remember your experience. Designate a specific sum for souvenirs to manage spending.
- Intra City Transport: Account for the cost of navigating around the Olympic venues and within the cities, which may include metro or bus fares. To conserve funds, consider investing in multi-day or unlimited travel passes.
- Travel Protection: Invest in travel insurance to safeguard against unexpected costs or emergencies, including medical situations, trip interruptions, lost belongings, and other contingencies. Evaluate various insurance options to find a plan that aligns with your requirements and financial plan.
- Service Appreciation: Prepare to leave tips for exemplary service in restaurants, cafes, or hotels, as is customary in France. Plan for these gratuities to show appreciation for good service, even though they are not obligatory.
- Financial Transactions: For international visitors, be mindful of currency exchange rates and potential fees for credit card usage or cash withdrawals. To reduce extra

charges, consider exchanging currency beforehand or using credit cards that do not impose foreign transaction fees.

By meticulously planning for these ancillary costs, you can enjoy a fulfilling and stress-free experience at the Paris 2024 Olympic Games. Prioritize your expenditures, prepare in advance, and seize every opportunity to discover the host cities and revel in the thrill of the Olympic competitions.

Packing Essentials for Paris

As the 2024 Olympic Games draw global attention to the illustrious City of Light, tourists will have the chance to delve into the unique charm of Paris. The city's impressive architectural wonders and its esteemed gastronomic offerings promise an unmatched experience. For an authentic taste of Parisian joy, thoughtful packing is crucial, blending comfort with elegance. This detailed guide will reveal the key to mastering Parisian elegance with ease, providing the must-have items for exploring the city's picturesque districts, historic sites, and dynamic cultural hubs. Competitors and fans alike will find this selection invaluable for experiencing the Parisian lifestyle to the fullest during the Games.

We will suggest adaptable apparel that suits both daytime explorations and evening events, along with supportive footwear for strolling along the alluring boulevards of Paris. Our advice will help you pack both lightly and fashionably, ready to fully enjoy this remarkable occasion. Beyond style, Paris is a celebration of life's luxuries. Our guide will point out the indispensable accessories that will enhance your time in Paris, from refined carryalls to trendy eyewear that will merge you seamlessly with the city's inhabitants.

Additionally, we will provide pro tips on the essentials for the Olympic settings, ensuring you're geared up for the dynamic environment and the memorable experiences that lie ahead. From pocket-sized binoculars for close-up action to elegant yet practical rainwear for those surprise downpours, we have considered everything.

Join in the excitement of Paris and the Olympic Games with our carefully crafted packing guide. Discover the formula for traversing this mesmerizing city with poise, flair, and an adventurous spirit. Prepare to forge unforgettable memories that encapsulate the spirit of this unparalleled event in one of the globe's most enchanting metropolises.

Weather and climate considerations (clothing and gear)

When preparing for the 2024 Paris Olympics, it's crucial to consider the city's diverse weather patterns. This comprehensive guide outlines the essentials for your wardrobe and accessories.

Climate Considerations for Paris in Summer

The Olympics will coincide with the peak of summer, a period characterized by warm, sunny days in Paris, with temperatures averaging between 64°F (18°C) and 77°F (25°C). Despite this, the weather can fluctuate, leading to occasional rain and cooler temperatures.

The Importance of Layering

Adapting to the unpredictable summer climate in Paris requires strategic layering. Opt for light, airy garments such as cotton or linen tops, shirts, and dresses. Include some long-sleeve options for when the temperature drops. A compact, lightweight jacket or blazer is also wise for sudden downpours or brisk evenings.

Rain Preparedness

Brief rain showers are not uncommon in Parisian summers, so it's prudent to pack a foldable travel umbrella or a light raincoat that's breathable and easy to carry.

Footwear for Comfort

Given the extensive walking you'll do while exploring Paris and attending Olympic events, prioritize comfortable footwear. Choose sneakers or walking shoes with ample cushioning and support. Wear them prior to your journey to prevent blisters. Having multiple pairs to alternate can be beneficial, and for more relaxed outings, sandals or canvas slip-ons are perfect.

Sun Protection Measures

The Parisian summer sun calls for adequate protection: include a hat with a wide brim or a cap, UV-blocking sunglasses, and sunscreen with a high SPF. Clothing with UPF (UV protection factor) is also advisable for those long hours outdoors.

Olympic Event Accessories

To enhance your Olympic experience, carry a small backpack or crossbody bag for essentials like snacks, water, portable chargers, and compact binoculars. A lightweight, waterproof poncho or blanket is useful for outdoor seating. Sunglasses and a hat are essential for daytime competitions.

Evening Attire

For evening events, consider packing dressier yet casual attire such as sundresses, slacks, or collared shirts. Adding a lightweight blazer or cardigan can elevate your look while maintaining comfort. Equipped with a carefully curated selection of breathable layers, rain gear, supportive footwear, and sun protection, you'll be well-prepared to fully enjoy the 2024 Paris Olympics in style and comfort, regardless of the weather conditions.

Essential Items for Attending the Paris 2024 Olympic Games

The anticipation of witnessing the Paris 2024 Olympic Games is thrilling, yet it's crucial to be thoroughly prepared for a seamless and delightful journey. Below is a detailed checklist of indispensable items to remember:

Admission and Identity Verification:

Olympic Passes: Secure your access to the events with your Olympic passes. Keep them in a safe, easily accessible place, either as physical copies or on your mobile device.

Identification: Carry a recognized photo ID (such as a passport for international visitors) for identity verification when retrieving tickets, entering venues, or during security procedures.

Travel and Event Details:

Travel Documentation: Have all necessary travel documents at hand, including a passport (with at least three months' validity post your planned return), any required visas, and insurance paperwork.

Event Schedule: Acquire and carry the official event schedule or information guides for the activities you're attending, noting locations, entry points, and start times.

Lodging Information: Keep your hotel or accommodation details, including the address, contact number, and reservation code, easily accessible.

Essentials for Personal Use:

Smartphone: An indispensable tool for communication, navigation, capturing memories, and accessing event updates. Ensure it's charged, and consider a local data plan for cost-effective usage.

Currency and Cards: Bring a reasonable amount of Euro cash for minor transactions and have debit/credit cards for more significant expenses, ticket retrieval, or ATM use.

Medication: Include any daily medications along with the corresponding prescriptions. Pack sufficient quantities for your entire visit.

Additional Suggested Items:

Eco-Friendly Water Container: Maintain hydration, particularly in the summer heat, with a refillable water bottle to minimize plastic waste and expenses.

Sun Protection: Arm yourself with sunscreen (SPF 30+) and a brimmed hat for defense against the sun's rays.

Protective Eyewear: Shield your eyes with sunglasses to combat the sun's brightness.

Hand Cleanser: Keep a travel-sized hand sanitizer for clean hands, especially when soap and water are scarce.

Emergency Charger: A portable battery pack is invaluable for ensuring your phone remains operational, particularly during heavy use.

Compact Bag: A small backpack or crossbody bag is practical for carrying water, sunscreen, guides, and your phone while keeping your hands free.

Pre-Departure Tips:

Air Travel Guidelines: Familiarize yourself with your airline's luggage policy and rules regarding liquids and banned items to prevent airport troubles.

Final Verification: Prior to departing for the Games, confirm that you've packed all the essentials and have all the needed documents ready.

Equipped with these essential items, you're set for a trouble-free and memorable time at the Paris 2024 Olympic Games, enabling you to concentrate on enjoying this extraordinary international sports celebration.

Health and Safety Essentials for the Paris 2024 Olympics

Embarking on the journey to the Paris 2024 Olympics is set to be a thrilling escapade. However, safeguarding your health and security must take precedence. Below is a detailed inventory of vital provisions to carry along, guaranteeing a secure and pleasant visit:

Sun Protection Essentials:

Sunscreen: Choose a sunscreen offering SPF 30 or more, with comprehensive UVA/UVB protection and resistance to water. Reapply bi-hourly, particularly post-swimming or perspiration.

Protective Hat: A hat with a generous brim can defend your facial and neck areas from the sun. Select lightweight fabrics such as straw or cotton for comfort in the heat.

UV-blocking Sunglasses: Carry sunglasses that provide UV protection to safeguard your eyes against intense sunlight and UV exposure.

Hydration and Cleanliness Supplies:

Eco-friendly Water Container: It's essential to keep hydrated, more so in hot climates. Bring an eco-friendly water container to refill as needed and help minimize plastic waste.

Hand Cleanser: Keep a portable hand sanitizer on hand for maintaining cleanliness, especially when hand washing facilities are scarce at crowded venues or while touring the city.

Moist Towelettes: Include a compact pack of moist towelettes for quick clean-ups or a refreshing wipe-down during the day.

Lip Moisturizer: A hydrating lip balm can prevent your lips from becoming chapped due to dry, summery conditions.

Personal Care Items: Bring along your favorite compact toiletries and any personal care essentials you might need during your travels.

First-aid Necessities:

Prepare a small but comprehensive first-aid kit with items to manage minor injuries, including:

Adhesive Strips: A variety of bandages for different sized cuts and abrasions.

Antiseptic Towelettes: For cleansing small wounds and averting infection.

Pain Alleviators: Non-prescription pain medication such as acetaminophen or ibuprofen for relieving headaches or muscle discomfort.

Allergy Medication: Antihistamines can be a lifesaver if you suffer from seasonal allergies.

Extra Precautions:

Prescription Medicines: Ensure you have an adequate supply of any prescribed medications, along with a doctor's note if necessary.

Bug Repellent: If you're planning to spend time in outdoor spaces like parks or gardens, especially during evening hours, consider bringing along insect repellent.

Supportive Footwear: Wearing supportive and comfortable shoes is key for extensive walking, whether sightseeing or attending Olympic events, to prevent soreness and blisters.

Additional Tips:

Check Rules: Familiarize yourself with the guidelines concerning liquids and permitted items in both airlines and event venues to sidestep any security snags.

Tailor Your Kit: Modify this checklist according to your personal health requirements and conditions. Seek medical advice prior to your trip if you have any health-related questions.

Equipped with these crucial health and safety items, you'll be prepared to swiftly handle minor health concerns and enjoy a stress-free experience at the Paris 2024 Olympic Games. Immerse yourself in the excitement of the Games while keeping your health at the forefront for an unforgettable adventure.

Staying Safe and Healthy in Paris

The excitement surrounding the Paris 2024 Olympic Games is palpable, offering the promise of a memorable experience. However, prioritizing your health and safety during your stay is of utmost importance. This section provides vital information on how to maintain safety and wellness as you take in the enchanting ambiance of Paris.

In the Event of an Emergency: Essential Contact Information and Protocols in Paris

The Paris 2024 Olympic Games are anticipated to be secure and pleasurable, yet it's imperative to be equipped for any unexpected events. Below is a compilation of crucial emergency contacts and protocols to keep in mind:

Emergency Contact Numbers:

For immediate help in emergencies such as fires, medical crises, or to request police assistance, dial 112 from any phone. This service is complimentary and will direct you to the necessary emergency responders.

For non-urgent matters or issues related to tourism, reach out to the Tourist Police at +33 1 44 17 36 16. They provide support to visitors in several languages, including English.

Additional Support:

American nationals should save the contact details of the U.S. Embassy in Paris and the nearest U.S. Consulate to their phones for assistance with lost passports, medical emergencies, or legal matters.

U.S. Embassy Paris: +33 1 43 12 22 22

U.S. Consulate General Marseille: +33 4 91 54 54 00 (most accessible consulate for Olympic visitors)

For those with travel insurance, ensure you are familiar with your provider's contact details and emergency procedures.

Safety Precautions:

- Stay vigilant and keep personal belongings like wallets and smartphones secure, especially in bustling areas.

- Guard against pickpockets by carrying minimal cash and storing important documents securely, particularly on public transport and at tourist sites.
- If a situation feels unsafe, trust your instincts and leave the area.
- In an emergency where language is a barrier, seek someone who can assist with communication.

Health Emergencies:

- A basic first-aid kit can be useful for minor injuries but is not a replacement for professional care.
- For medical advice or over-the-counter medication, visit a local pharmacy. In the case of more serious health concerns, head to the nearest hospital or urgent care center.
- Carry your health insurance card or documentation to expedite interactions with healthcare services.
- By acquainting yourself with these emergency contacts and protocols, you can better manage unexpected circumstances and access the help you may need while in Paris.

Remember: Caution and preparedness are key. Being well-informed and ready for various scenarios will enhance your peace of mind and contribute to a delightful experience at the Paris 2024 Olympic Games.

General Health and Safety Tips for Travelers in Paris

To ensure a seamless and pleasurable visit, particularly amid the lively environment of the 2024 Olympic Games in Paris, consider the following critical health and safety recommendations:

Pre-Departure Preparations:

- Conduct Thorough Research: Acquaint yourself with the cultural norms, legal stipulations, and potential health hazards prevalent in France. It may be beneficial to enroll with your nation's embassy or consulate for updates and support when necessary.
- Immunizations: Confirm that you are up to date with all necessary immunizations, including those for measles, mumps, rubella, and tetanus, as well as booster shots for diphtheria and polio.

- Secure Travel Insurance: Obtain comprehensive travel insurance that provides coverage for medical contingencies, trip interruptions, and possible losses.

Urban Safety:

- Stay Vigilant: Remain alert to your environment, particularly in high-traffic locations, safeguarding personal belongings such as wallets and smartphones.
- Honor Local Traditions: Dress conservatively at religious sites and show respect for local customs and manners to prevent cultural missteps.
- Emergency Contact: Store the universal emergency number (112) on your phone for quick access to fire, medical, or police aid.

Navigating Transportation:

- Public Transit Familiarity: Get to know the local transit system and secure your travel passes beforehand to circumvent delays and long lines.
- Taxi Usage: Opt for authorized taxi services and establish the fare before departure to prevent disputes.
- Bicycle Safety: If cycling, don a helmet and stick to bike lanes for increased protection.

Extra Advice:

- Basic French Communication: Mastering essential French expressions can greatly assist in interacting with residents and finding your way around.
- Offline Resources: Pre-download maps and translation tools onto your mobile device for use during loss of internet connectivity.
- Cash in Euros: Keep a reserve of Euros for minor transactions or in places where card payment is not an option.
- Anticipate Delays: Prepare for potential hold-ups, particularly during busy times and on days with scheduled events. Adapt with an open mind and savor the Parisian ambiance.

Staying Informed: Resources for Official Updates

Maintaining awareness of official communications and guidance during the Paris 2024 Olympic Games is essential for a seamless and pleasant visit. Here are a variety of dependable sources to keep you informed:

Primary Online Platforms and Mobile Applications:

Paris 2024 Olympic Games Official Site: The central repository for all pertinent details about the Games can be found at the official site (https://www.paris2024.org/en/). It provides the latest news regarding event schedules, venues, transit options, ticket sales, and visitor guidelines.

Paris 2024 Official Application: Install the official mobile application to receive instantaneous updates, interactive timetables, maps, and alerts on your smartphone, which is especially useful for city navigation and obtaining current information while on the move.

Digital Social Platforms:

Paris 2024 Social Media Presence: Engage with the official Paris 2024 Olympic Games social media profiles on platforms like Facebook, Twitter, and Instagram (@Paris2024) to receive prompt news, updates, and the opportunity to connect with fellow attendees.

Journalistic and Media Outlets:

Trusted News Outlets: Keep abreast of the Olympic Games by following credible news organizations, both domestic and global, known for their journalistic integrity and trustworthy reporting.

Tourist Support Services:

Paris Visitor Bureau Web Portal: The Paris Visitor Bureau's website (https://www.paristouristinformation.fr/) is a treasure trove of visitor information, providing insights on transit service interruptions, potential municipal shutdowns, and tips for city navigation during significant happenings such as the Olympics.

Visitor Information Booths: Seek out visitor information booths across Paris for support and printed resources like maps and brochures with the latest official advisories and news.

Additional Recommendations:

Newsletter Subscriptions: Subscribe to official newsletters from the Paris 2024 organizers or local tourism boards to have the latest updates and guidelines delivered straight to your email.

Overcoming Language Hurdles: Should you face language challenges, make use of translation applications or request help from information kiosks or hotel personnel to comprehend official communications and advisories.

By actively engaging with these channels and keeping abreast of official communications, you can traverse the city with assurance and make well-informed choices during your stay in Paris for the 2024 Olympic Games. Remember, being well-informed is key to amplifying your experience and ensuring a secure and delightful trip.

Cultural Exchange Tips and Overcoming Language Barriers

The 2024 Olympic Games in Paris present an extraordinary chance not only to observe elite athletic performances but also to engage with the city's vibrant cultural fabric. This section provides practical advice to help you navigate cultural interactions and surmount linguistic challenges, deepening your bond with both the city and its residents.

Cultivate Openness and Respect:

Embrace Diversity: Enter conversations with Parisians with an open heart and a keen interest in their way of life, embracing the diversity you come across to enhance your appreciation of the local culture.

Polite Interaction: Pay attention to how you use gestures and the tone of your voice, striving for polite and considerate exchanges. A basic "Bonjour" or "Bonsoir" can be instrumental in fostering a friendly connection.

Acquaint Yourself with Basic French:

Key Phrases: Mastering simple French expressions beyond basic salutations can greatly improve your interactions, making connections more meaningful. Learn phrases such as "Merci," "S'il vous plaît," "Excusez-moi," and "Parlez-vous anglais?"

Non-verbal Signals: When your French is limited, rely on non-verbal communication like hand gestures and facial expressions. A warm smile and a kind gesture can transcend language barriers and show your earnest efforts.

Engage with Cultural Offerings:

Local Gastronomy: Step off the beaten path to taste genuine Parisian dishes in neighborhood cafés, patisseries, and markets. This allows you to savor French gastronomy and partake in the country's cultural heritage.

Art and History Immersion: By visiting museums, historical monuments, and cultural sites, you gain insight into France's history and artistic legacy, which can also serve as a catalyst for insightful discussions and cultural connections.

Addressing Language Hurdles:

Translation Technology: Make use of dependable translation applications to help with language difficulties when needed. These aids can support basic exchanges and promote understanding.

Phrasebook in Hand: Keep a compact French phrasebook handy as a useful aid for learning phrases and managing straightforward dialogues.

Embrace the Learning Process: Don't let language obstacles deter you. View them as chances to grow and engage meaningfully with Parisians. Even modest attempts at French can be well-received and lead to gratifying exchanges.

Additional Recommendations:

Appropriate Attire: Dressing conservatively, particularly when visiting sacred sites, is a sign of respect for local customs and sensibilities in this cosmopolitan setting.

Patience and Empathy: Communication might require extra time and patience, especially with limited language ability. Show patience and gratitude for the efforts made by locals in communicating with you.

By adopting an attitude of curiosity, respect, and cultural empathy, and by proactively addressing language barriers, you can unlock a more profound and unforgettable Parisian experience during the Olympic Games. Seize this chance to connect with the city and its people, and you will uncover the true essence of cultural exchange, leaving an indelible impact on both yourself and those you meet.

Celebrating Diversity and Sportsmanship at the Olympics

The 2024 Paris Olympics are set to be not just a display of athletic skill but a worldwide festivity of cultural variety and the ethos of sportsmanship. Competitors from across the globe will converge in the City of Light, each bringing their unique heritage, ethnicity, and personal story, to partake in contests marked by fairness and mutual admiration.

Showcasing Diversity:

A Worldwide Celebration: The Olympic stage is a canvas for countries to exhibit their distinct cultural signatures. The sight of athletes donning national costumes, the sound of anthems resonating with national pride, and the dynamic presence of diverse supporters all contribute to an authentically international ambiance.

Overcoming Divides: The Olympics are a testament to inclusiveness and the unifying power of sports across cultural and societal divides. The presence of athletes with disabilities competing on equal footing with others, and the growing number of female participants in sports once dominated by men, reflect the forward-thinking ethos of the Olympic movement.

Harmony Amidst Competition: Although the essence of the Olympics is competitive, it also cultivates a harmony found in diversity. Competitors from varied nations interact with mutual respect and friendship, often building bonds that surpass geopolitical lines.

The Pillars of Sportsmanship:

Honoring the Competitor: The true essence of victory is not merely in triumph but in triumph with respect for one's competitors. Acknowledging an opponent's prowess, offering solace in defeat, and the exchange of handshakes are all manifestations of the Olympic spirit.

Integrity in Competition: The Olympic ethos is deeply rooted in playing by the rules and maintaining the highest standards of fair play. Those athletes who compete with honor under intense pressure are revered and epitomize the noble nature of sports.

Dignity in Triumph and Adversity: The Olympics are a stage for jubilation and sorrow alike. Athletes who celebrate their victories modestly and those who accept defeat with dignity exemplify the true spirit of sportsmanship.

A Collective Celebration:

Cultural Interaction: The Olympics are a rare chance for cross-cultural engagement. Encouraging athletes from different nations, indulging in global gastronomy, and interacting with international fans are part of the rich Olympic experience.

Motivating Future Champions: The commitment, resilience, and fair play demonstrated by Olympic athletes serve as a source of motivation for the youth, encouraging them to value physical activity, teamwork, and the pursuit of excellence. The Paris 2024 Olympic Games are emblematic of unity within diversity, celebrating a myriad of cultures while promoting an ethos of sportsmanship. This global gathering transcends mere athletic contests, spreading a message of hope, inclusivity, and the best of human capacity.

Appendices

Important Contact Information: Paris 2024 Olympic Games

Organizers:
- **Paris 2024 Official Website:** https://www.paris2024.org/en/
- **Paris 2024 Contact Form:** https://press.paris2024.org/contacts/

Embassies and Consulates:
- **U.S. Embassy Paris:**
  - Phone: +33 1 43 12 22 22
  - Website: https://travel.state.gov/content/travel/en/international-travel/International-Travel-Country-Information-Pages/France.html
- **U.S. Consulate General Marseille:** (closest consulate to most Olympic attendees)
  - Phone: +33 4 91 54 54 00
  - Website: https://fr.usembassy.gov/

Local Emergency Services:
- **Emergency Services:** Dial **112** from any phone for immediate assistance in case of fire, medical emergencies, or police assistance.
- **Tourist Police:** +33 1 44 17 36 16 (for non-emergency situations or tourist-related issues)

Additional Resources:
- **Paris Tourist Office Website:** https://www.paristouristinformation.fr/
- **Travel Insurance Provider:** Contact information for your travel insurance provider in case of emergencies.

Official Websites:
- **Paris 2024 Olympic Games:** https://www.paris2024.org/en/ - The official website of the Paris 2024 Olympic Games, offering comprehensive information on schedules, venues, ticketing, transportation, and news updates.
- **Paris Tourist Office:** https://parisjetaime.com/eng/ - The official website of the Paris Tourist Office, providing essential information on attractions, transportation, accommodation, and events throughout the city.

Informational Websites:
- **France.fr:** https://www.france.fr/en - The official website of France Tourism, offering comprehensive information on tourist destinations, travel tips, and cultural insights.
- **The Local France:** https://www.thelocal.fr/category/france-news - An English-language news website offering local news and cultural insights for visitors and residents of France.

Transportation Resources:
- **RATP:** https://www.ratp.fr/en - The official website of the Parisian public transportation network (RATP) offering information on metro lines, bus routes, tickets, and journey planning.
- **Uber:** https://www.uber.com/ - A ridesharing app offering taxi-like services in major cities, including Paris.

Language Learning Resources:
- **Duolingo:** https://www.duolingo.com/ - A free language learning app offering gamified courses for various languages, including French.
- **Memrise:** https://www.memrise.com/ - Another free language learning app offering interactive and engaging courses for various languages, including French.

Additional Resources:
- **Lonely Planet Paris:** https://shop.lonelyplanet.com/products/paris - A popular travel guidebook offering comprehensive information on Paris, including attractions, transportation, and cultural insights.
- **Rick Steves Paris:** https://www.ricksteves.com/europe/france/paris - Another popular travel guidebook offering information and recommendations for planning your trip to Paris.

Remember:
- Store this information in your phone or carry a physical copy for easy access.
- Familiarize yourself with French emergency procedures before your trip.
- Download offline maps and translation apps to your phone in case you lose internet access.

By having this information readily available, you can navigate unforeseen situations with greater confidence and ensure a safe and enjoyable experience at the Paris 2024 Olympic Games.

Appendix B: Maps

Map 1: Charles De Gaulle Airport to Eiffel tower

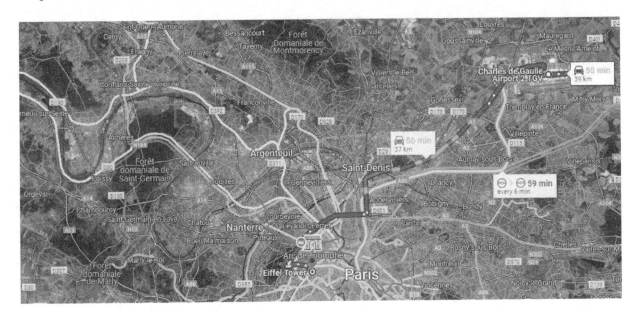

Map 2: Olympic Venues in Paris

Map 3: Restaurants

Map 4: Activities

Map 5: ATMs

This appendix provides a list of valuable resources and websites to enhance your experience at the Paris 2024 Olympic Games and in the city of Paris:

Remember: This list is not exhaustive, and numerous other resources are available online and in print. Explore these resources and discover more to enrich your experience in Paris and the 2024 Olympic Games.

Made in the USA
Monee, IL
27 July 2024

62708870R00090